T0244453

THE ROAD TO CALVARY

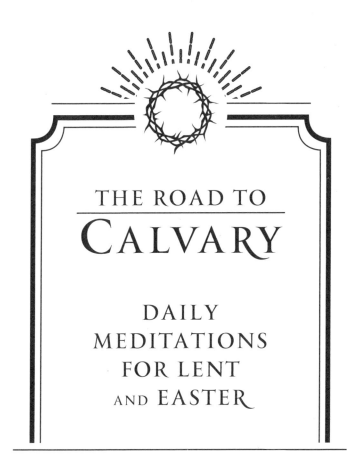

THE ROAD TO
CALVARY

DAILY
MEDITATIONS
FOR LENT
AND EASTER

ST. ALPHONSUS LIGUORI

TAN BOOKS
GASTONIA, NORTH CAROLINA

Originally published by Benziger Brothers, R. Washbourne, and M. H. Gill & Son as *The Passion and Death of Jesus Christ by St. Alphonsus de Liguori.* Retypeset, republished, updated with modern numerals, and edited by TAN Books in 2023 as *The Road to Calvary: Daily Meditations for Lent and Easter.*

Cover design by Caroline Green

ISBN: 978-1-5051-2678-5
Kindle ISBN: 978-1-5051-2679-2
ePUB ISBN: 978-1-5051-2680-8

Published in the United States by
TAN Books
PO Box 269
Gastonia, NC 28053
www.TANBooks.com

Printed in India

CONTENTS

Easter Meditations

Appendix

Publisher's Note

Saint Alphonsus de Liguori (1696–1787) was an Italian Catholic bishop, spiritual writer, composer, musician, artist, poet, lawyer, scholastic philosopher, and theologian. He also founded the Congregation of the Most Holy Redeemer, known as the Redemptorists, in 1732. He was one of the most prolific writers in the history of the Catholic Church and was later declared a doctor of the Church and the patron of moral theologians. TAN Books is pleased to present this book, *The Road to Calvary: Daily Meditations for Lent and Easter* from the original book entitled *The Passion and Death of Jesus Christ*.

Few saints have written with such love, depth, and simplicity on Christ, Our Lady, the mysteries of our Faith, and especially the sufferings of Christ as Saint Alphonsus de Liguori. Meditating on the passion and death of Jesus is the surest path to virtue and holiness. As Saint Alphonsus so beautifully wrote, "Who, then, can ever complain that he suffers wrongfully, when he considers Jesus, who was *bruised for our sins*? Who can refuse to obey, on account of some inconvenience, when Jesus *became obedient unto death?* Who can refuse ignominies, when he beholds Jesus treated as a fool, as a mock king, as a disorderly person; struck, spit upon His face, and suspended upon an infamous gibbet?"

TAN Books is pleased to present this little work for the first time to join several other TAN works by Saint Alphonsus, such as *The Glories of Mary, Preparation for Death,* and *Visits to the Blessed Sacrament.*

May you, dear reader, prepare your heart for the passion, death, and resurrection of Jesus through these powerful daily Lenten and Easter meditations. The road to Calvary begins and ends with prayer.

The Publisher

LENTEN
MEDITATIONS

THE VALUE OF MEDITATING ON THE PASSION

"He who desires," says Saint Bonaventure, "to go on advancing from virtue to virtue, from grace to grace, should meditate continually on the Passion of Jesus." And he adds that "there is no practice more profitable for the entire sanctification of the soul than the frequent meditation of the sufferings of Jesus Christ."

Saint Augustine also said that a single tear shed at the remembrance of the passion of Jesus is worth more than a pilgrimage to Jerusalem, or a year of fasting on bread and water. Yes, because it was for this end that our Savior suffered so much: in order that we should think of His sufferings; because if we think on them, it is impossible not to be inflamed with divine love: *The charity of Christ presses us,*[1] says Saint Paul. Jesus is loved

---

[1]   2 Cor. 5:14.

by few, because few consider the pains He has suffered for us, but he that frequently considers them cannot live without loving Jesus. "The charity of Christ presses us." He will feel himself so constrained by His love that he will not find it possible to refrain from loving a God so full of love, who has suffered so much to make us love Him.

Therefore the Apostle said that he desired to know nothing but Jesus, and Jesus crucified—that is, the love that He has shown us on the cross: *I judged not myself to know anything among you but Jesus Christ, and Him crucified.*[2] And, in truth, from what books can we better learn the science of the saints—that is, the science of loving God—than from Jesus crucified? That great servant of God, Brother Bernard of Corlione, the Capuchin, not being able to read, his brother religious wanted to teach him, upon which he went to consult his crucifix, but Jesus answered him from the cross, "What is reading? What are books? Behold, I am the book wherein you may continually read the love I have borne you." O great subject to be considered during our whole life and during all eternity! A God dead for the love of us! A God dead for the love of us! O wonderful subject!

Saint Thomas Aquinas was one day paying a visit to Saint Bonaventure and asked him from what book he had drawn all the beautiful lessons he had written. Saint Bonaventure showed him the image of the Crucified, which was completely blackened by all the kisses that he had given it, and said, "This is my book

---

[2] 1 Cor. 2:2.

whence I receive everything that I write; and it has taught me whatever little I know."

In short, all the saints have learned the art of loving God from the study of the crucifix. Brother John of Alvernia, every time that he beheld Jesus wounded, could not restrain his tears. Brother James of Tuderto, when he heard the passion of our Redeemer read, not only wept bitterly, but broke out into loud sobs, overcome with the love with which he was inflamed toward his beloved Lord.

MEDITATION 2: THURSDAY AFTER ASH WEDNESDAY

THE LOVE OF JESUS CHRIST

We read in history of a proof of love so prodigious that it will be the admiration of all ages. There was once a king, lord of many kingdoms, who had one only son, so beautiful, so holy, so amiable that he was the delight of his father, who loved him as much as himself. This young prince had a great affection for one of his slaves, so much so that, the slave having committed a crime for which he had been condemned to death, the prince offered himself to die for the slave; the father, being jealous of justice, was satisfied to condemn his beloved son to death in order that the slave might remain free from the punishment that he deserved, and thus the son died a malefactor's death, and the slave was freed from punishment.

This fact, the like of which has never happened in this world, and never will happen, is related in the Gospels, where we read that the Son of God, the Lord of the universe, seeing that man was condemned to eternal death in punishment of his sins, chose to take upon Himself human flesh, and thus to pay by His death the penalty due to man: *He was offered because it was His own will.*[3] And His Eternal Father caused Him to die upon the cross to save us miserable sinners: *He spared not His own Son, but delivered Him up for us all.*[4] What do you think, O devout soul, of this love of the Son and of the Father?

You, then, O my beloved Redeemer, choose by Your death to sacrifice Yourself in order to obtain the pardon of my sins. And what return of gratitude shall I then make to You? You have done too much to oblige me to love You; I should indeed be most ungrateful to You if I did not love You with my whole heart. You have given for me Your divine life; I, miserable sinner that I am, give You my own life. Yes, I will at least spend that period of life that remains to me only in loving You, obeying You, and pleasing You.

O men, men, let us love this our Redeemer, who, being God, has not disdained to take upon Himself our sins in order to satisfy by His sufferings for the chastisement which we have deserved: *Surely He has borne our infirmities and carried our sorrows.*[5] Saint Augustine says that Our Lord, in creating us, formed us by virtue of His power, but in redeeming us, He has saved us from death by means of His sufferings: "He created us in His strength; He sought us back in His weakness."[6]

---

[3]   Is. 53:7.
[4]   Rom. 8:32.
[5]   Is. 53:4.
[6]   *In Joannem*, tractus 15.

How much do I not owe You, O Jesus my Savior! Oh, if I were to give my blood a thousand times over—if I were to spend a thousand lives for You—it would yet be nothing. Oh, how could anyone that meditated much on the love which You have shown him in Your passion love anything else but You? Through the love with which You loved us on the cross, grant me the grace to love You with my whole heart. I love You, infinite Goodness; I love You above every other good, and I ask nothing more of You but Your holy love.

JESUS CHOSE TO SUFFER (PART I)

"Two things," says Cicero, "make us know a lover—that he does good to his beloved and that he suffers torments for him, and this last is the greatest sign of true love." God has indeed already shown His love to man by many benefits bestowed upon him, but His love would not have been satisfied by only doing good to man, as says Saint Peter Chrysologus, if He had not found the means to prove to him how much He loved him by also suffering and dying for him, as He did by taking upon Him human flesh: "But He held it to be little if He showed His love without suffering,"[7] and what greater means could God have discovered to prove to us the immense love which He bears us than by making Himself man and suffering for us? "In no other

---

[7]   *Serm.* 69.

way could the love of God towards us be shown," writes Saint Gregory Nazianzen.

My beloved Jesus, how much have You labored to show me Your love and to make me enamored of Your goodness! Great indeed, then, would be the injury I should do You if I were to love You but little, or to love anything else but You.

Ah, when He showed Himself to us, a God wounded, crucified, and dying, did He not indeed (says Cornelius à Lapide) give us the greatest proofs of the love that He bears us? "God showed His utmost love on the cross."[8] And before him, St. Bernard said that Jesus, in His passion, showed us that His love towards us could not be greater than it was: "In the shame of the Passion is shown the greatest and incomparable love."[9] The Apostle writes that when Jesus Christ chose to die for our salvation, then appeared how far the love of God extended towards us miserable creatures: *The goodness and kindness of God our Savior appeared.*[10]

O my most loving Savior! I feel indeed that all Your wounds speak to me of the love that You bear me. And who that had so many proofs of Your love could resist loving You in return? Saint Teresa was indeed right, O most amiable Jesus, when she said that he who loves You not gives a proof that he does not know You.

---

[8]   In 1 Cor. 1:25.
[9]   *De Passione* c. 41.
[10] Titus 3:4.

JESUS CHOSE TO SUFFER (PART 2)

Jesus Christ could easily have obtained for us salvation without suffering, and in leading a life of ease and delight, but no, Saint Paul says, *having joy set before Him, He endured the cross.*[11] He refused the riches, the delights, the honors of the world, and chose for Himself a life of poverty and a death full of suffering and ignominy. And wherefore? Would it not have sufficed for Him to have offered to His eternal Father one single prayer for the pardon of man? For this prayer, being of infinite value, would have been sufficient to save the world, and infinite worlds besides. Why, then, did He choose for Himself so much suffering, and a death so cruel, that an author has said very truly that through mere pain the soul of Jesus separated itself from His

---

[11]   Heb. 12:2.

body?[12] To what purpose so much cost in order to save man? Saint John Chrysostom answers, a single prayer of Jesus would indeed have sufficed to redeem us, but it was not sufficient to show us the love that our God has borne us: "That which sufficed to redeem us was not sufficient for love." And Saint Thomas confirms this when he says, "Christ, in suffering from love and obedience offered to God more than the expiation of the offence of the human race demanded."[13] Because Jesus loved us so much, He desired to be loved very much by us, and therefore He did everything that He could, even unto suffering for us, in order to conciliate our love and to show that there was nothing more that He could do to make us love Him: "He endured much weariness," says Saint Bernard, "that He might bind man to love Him much."[14]

And what greater proof of love, says our Savior Himself, can a friend show towards the person he loves than to give his life for his sake? *Greater love than this no man has, that a man lay down his life for his friends.*[15] But You, O most loving Jesus, says Saint Bernard, have done more than this, since You have given Your life for us, who were not Your friends, but Your enemies and rebels against You: "You have a greater charity, Lord, in giving Your life for Your enemies."[16] And this is what the Apostle

[12]   Vincent Contenson, *Theologia Mentis et Cordis*, I. 10, d. 4, c. 1, sp. 1.
[13]   *Summa Theologica*, III, q. 48. a. 2.
[14]   *In Canticum Canticorum*, sermo 11.
[15]   John 15:13.
[16]   *Sermo de Passione Domini.*

observes when he writes, *He commends His charity towards us, because when as yet we were sinners, according to the time, Christ died for us.*[17]

You would then die for me, Your enemy, O my Jesus, and yet can I resist so much love? Behold, here I am; since You so anxiously desire that I should love You, I will drive away every other love from my breast and will love You alone.

---

[17]   Rom. 5:8–9.

MEDITATION 5: FIRST SUNDAY OF LENT

THE PRINCIPAL END OF THE PASSION

Saint John Chrysostom says that the principal end Jesus had in His passion was to discover to us His love, and thus to draw our hearts to Himself by the remembrance of the pains that He endured for us: "This was the principal cause of the passion of our Lord; He wished it to be known how great was the love of God for man—of God, who would rather be loved than feared."[18] Saint Thomas adds that we may, through the passion of Jesus, know the greatness of the love that God bears to man: "By this man understands the greatness of the love of God to man."[19] And Saint John had said before, *In this we have known the charity of God, because He has laid down His life for us.*[20]

[18]   *De Pau.* s. 6.
[19]   *S. T.,* III, q. 46, a. 3.
[20]   1 Jn. 3:16.

O my Jesus, Immaculate Lamb sacrificed on the cross for me, let not all that You have suffered for me be lost, but accomplish in me the object of Your great sufferings! Oh, bind me entirely with the sweet chains of Your love in order that I may not leave You and that I may nevermore be separated from You: "Most sweet Jesus, suffer me not to be separated from You; suffer me not to be separated from You."

Saint Luke relates that Moses and Elias on Mount Tabor, speaking of the passion of Jesus Christ, called it an excess: *And they spoke of His excess that He should accomplish in Jerusalem.*[21] "Yes," says Saint Bonaventure, and rightly was the passion of Jesus called an excess; for "it was an excess of suffering and an excess of love." And a devout author adds, "What more could He suffer that He has not endured? The excess of His love reached the highest point."[22] Yes, indeed; for the divine law imposes on men no other obligation than that of loving their neighbors as themselves, but Jesus has loved man more than Himself: "He loved these more than Himself," says Saint Cyril.

You, then, O my beloved Redeemer—I will say to You with Saint Augustine—loved me more than Yourself since to save me You would lose Your divine life—a life infinitely more precious than the lives of all men and angels put together. You loved me more than Yourself because You were willing to die for me.[23]

21 Luke 9:31.
22 Vincent Contenson, *Theologia Mentis et Cordis*, I. 10, d. 4, c. 1, sp. 1.
23 *Sol. an. ad D. c. xiii.*

O infinite God, exclaims the Abbot Guerric, You have for the love of men (if it is lawful to say so) become prodigal of Yourself. "Yes, indeed," he adds, "since You have not been satisfied with bestowing Your gifts, but You have also given Yourself to recover lost man."[24] O prodigy, O excess of love, worthy only of infinite goodness!

"And who," says Saint Thomas of Villanova, "will ever be able, Lord, to understand even in the slightest degree the immensity of Your love in having loved us miserable worms so much that You chose to die, even upon a cross, for us?" "Oh, how this love," continues the same saint, "exceeds all measure, all understanding!"[25]

---

[24]   *In Pentecosten*, sermo 1.
[25]   *In Nativitate Domini*, concio 3.

MEDITATION 6: FIRST MONDAY OF LENT

THE FOOLISHNESS OF GOD

But faith teaches us that Jesus has really undertaken and accomplished this great work of redemption which the Gentiles esteemed and called folly. "We have seen," says St. Laurence Justinian, "Eternal Wisdom, the only-begotten of God, become as it were a fool through the excessive love He bears man."[26] Yes, adds Cardinal Hugo, for it seemed nothing but a folly that a God should choose to die for men: "It seemed a folly that God should die for the salvation of men."[27]

Giacopone, who in this world had been a man of letters, and afterwards became a Franciscan, seemed to have become mad through the love that he bore to Jesus Christ. One day Jesus appeared to him and said, "Giacopone, why do you commit these follies?" "Why," he answered, "because You have taught them to me. If I am mad," said he, "You have been more mad

---

[26]   *Sermo de Nativitate Domini.*
[27]   *Commentary on 1 Cor. 4.*

than I, in that You have died for me. I am a fool, for You have been a greater fool."

Thus, also, Saint Mary Magdalene of Pazzi, being in an ecstasy, exclaimed, "O God of love! O God of love! The love that You bear to creatures, O my Jesus, is too great indeed." And one day, when quite enraptured, she took an image of the Crucified and began running about the monastery, crying, "O Love! Love! I shall never rest, my God, from calling You Love." Then turning to the religious, she said, "Do you not know, my dear sisters, that Jesus Christ is nothing but love? He is even mad with love, and I will go on saying it continually." And she added that she wished she could be heard by the whole universe when she called Jesus "Love" in order that the love of Jesus might be known and loved by all. And she sometimes even began to ring the bell in order that all the people in the world should come (as she desired, if it had been possible) to love her Jesus.

Yes, my sweetest Redeemer, permit me to say so, this Your spouse was indeed right when she called You mad with love. And does it not indeed seem a folly that You should choose to die for love of me, for so ungrateful a worm as I am, and whose offenses You foresaw, as well as the infidelities of which I should be guilty? But if You, my God, are thus become mad, as it were, for the love of me, how is it that I do not become mad for the love of a God? When I have seen You crucified and dead for me, how is it that I can think of any other than You? Yes, O my Lord, my sovereign good, more worthy of love than every other good, I love You more than myself. I promise for the future to love none other but You and to think constantly on the love You have shown me by dying in the midst of so many sufferings for me. O scourges, O thorns, O nails, O cross, O wounds, O sufferings, O death of my Savior! You irresistibly constrain me to love Him who has so much loved me. O Incarnate Word, O loving God! My soul is enamored with You. I would fain love You so much that I should find no pleasure but in pleasing You, my most sweet Lord, and since You so earnestly desire my love, I protest that I will only live for You. I desire to do whatever You will of me. O my Jesus! I pray You, help me, and grant that I may please You entirely and continually in time and in eternity. Mary, my Mother, entreat Jesus for me in order that He may grant me His holy love, for I desire nothing else in this world and in the next but to love Jesus. Amen.

MEDITATION 7: FIRST TUESDAY OF LENT

JESUS SUFFERS FROM THE BEGINNING OF HIS LIFE

The divine Word came into the world and took upon Himself human flesh in order to make Himself loved of man, and therefore He came with such a longing to suffer for our sake that He would not lose a moment in beginning to torment Himself, at least by apprehension. Hardly was He conceived in the womb of Mary when He represented to His mind all the sufferings of His passion, and in order to obtain for us pardon and divine grace, He offered Himself to His eternal Father to satisfy for us through His dolors all the chastisements due to our sins, and from that moment, He began to suffer everything that He afterwards endured in His most bitter death.

O my most loving Redeemer! What have I hitherto done or suffered for You? If I could for a thousand years endure for Your sake all the torments that all the martyrs have suffered, they would yet be nothing compared with that one first moment in which You offered Yourself and began to suffer for me.

The martyrs did indeed suffer great pains and ignominy, but they only endured them at the time of their martyrdom. Jesus, even from the first instant of His life, continually suffered all the torments of His passion; for, from the first moment, He had before His eyes all the horrid scene of torments and insults which He was to receive from men. Wherefore He said by the mouth of the prophet, *My sorrow is continually before me.*[28] O my Jesus! You have been so desirous to suffer for my sake that You would even endure Your sufferings before the time, and yet I am so desirous after the pleasures of this world. How many times have I offended You in order to please my body! O my Lord! Through the merits of Your sufferings, take away from me, I beseech You, all affection for earthly pleasures. For Your love I desire to abstain from this satisfaction.

God, in His compassion for us, does not generally reveal to us the trials that await us before the time when we are destined to endure them. If a criminal who is executed on a gibbet had had revealed to him from the first use of his reason the torture that awaited him, could he even have been capable of joy? If Saul from the beginning of his reign had had present to his mind the sword that was to pierce him, if Judas had foreseen the cord that was to suffocate him—how bitter would their lives have been!

---

[28] Ps. 37:18.

Our kind Redeemer, even from the first instant of His life, had always present before Him the scourges, the thorns, the cross, the outrages of His passion, the desolate death that awaited Him. When He beheld the victims which were sacrificed in the temple, He well knew that they were figures of the sacrifice which He, the Immaculate Lamb, would one day consummate on the altar of the cross. When He beheld the city of Jerusalem, He well knew that He was there to lose His life in a sea of sorrows and reproaches. When He saw His dear Mother, He already imagined that He saw her in an agony of suffering at the foot of the cross, near His dying self.

So that, O my Jesus, the horrible sight of all these evils kept You during the whole of Your life continually tormented and afflicted before the time of Your death. And You accepted and suffered everything for my sake. O my agonizing Lord! The sight alone of all the sins of the world, especially of mine, by which You already foresaw I should offend You, rendered Your life more afflicted and painful than all the lives that ever have been or ever will be. But, O my God, in what barbarous law is it written that a God should have so great love for a creature, and yet that creature should live without loving his God, or rather should offend and displease Him? O my Lord, make me know the greatness of Your love in order that I may no longer be ungrateful to You. Oh, if I but loved You, my Jesus—if I really loved You—how sweet it would be to me to suffer for You!

MEDITATION 8: FIRST WEDNESDAY OF LENT

JESUS'S SUFFERINGS COMPARED TO OURS

Jesus appeared one day on the cross to Sister Magdalene Orsini, who had been suffering for some time from some great affliction, and animated her to suffer it in peace. The servant of God answered, "But, Lord, You only hung on the cross for three hours, whereas I have gone on suffering this pain for several years." Jesus Christ then said to her reproachingly, "O ignorant that you are, what do you mean? From the first moment that I was in My Mother's womb, I suffered in My heart all that I afterwards endured on the cross."

And I, my dear Redeemer, how can I, at the sight of such great sufferings which You endured for my sake, during Your whole life, complain of those crosses which You send me for my good? I thank You for having redeemed me with so much love and such sufferings. In order to animate me to suffer with patience the pains of this life, You took upon Yourself all our evils. O my Lord, grant that Your sorrows may be ever present to my mind in order that I may always accept and desire to suffer for Your love.

Great as the sea is Your destruction.[29] The waters of the sea are all salt and bitter, so the life of Jesus Christ was full of bitterness and void of all consolation, as He Himself declared to Saint Margaret of Cortona. Moreover, as all the waters of the earth unite in the sea, so did all the sufferings of men unite in Jesus Christ; wherefore He said by the mouth of the Psalmist, *Save me, O God, for the waters are come in even unto my soul. . . . I am come into the depth of the sea, and a tempest has overwhelmed me.*[30] Save Me, O God, for sorrows have entered even the inmost parts of My soul, and I am left submerged in a tempest of ignominy and of sufferings, both interior and exterior.

O my dearest Jesus, my love, my life, my all, if I behold from without Your sacred body, I see nothing else but wounds. But if I enter into Your desolate heart, I find nothing but bitterness and sorrows, which made You suffer the agonies of death. O my Lord, and who but You, who are infinite goodness, would ever suffer so much and die for one of Your creatures? But because You are God, You love as a God alone can love, with a love which cannot be equaled by any other love.

---

[29]   Lam. 2:13.
[30]   Ps. 68:2–3.

Saint Bernard says, "In order to redeem the slave, the Father did not spare His own Son, nor did the Son spare Himself."[31] O infinite love of God! On the one hand the eternal Father required of Jesus Christ to satisfy for all the sins of men: *The Lord has laid on Him the iniquity of us all.*[32] On the other hand, Jesus, in order to save men in the most loving way that He could, chose to take upon Himself the utmost penalty due to divine justice for our sins. Wherefore, as Saint Thomas asserts, He took upon Himself in the highest degree all the sufferings and outrages that ever were borne. It was on this account that Isaiah called Him *a man of sorrows, despised, and the most abject of men.*[33] And with reason; for Jesus was tormented in all the members and senses of His body, and was still more bitterly afflicted in all the powers of His soul, so that the internal pains which He endured infinitely surpassed His external sufferings. Behold Him, then, torn, bloodless, treated as an impostor, as a sorcerer, a madman, abandoned even by His friends, and finally persecuted by all, until He finished His life upon an infamous gibbet. *Know you what I have done to you?*[34]

---

[31]   *Sermo de Passione Domini.*
[32]   Is. 53:6.
[33]   Is. 53:3.
[34]   John 13:12.

MEDITATION 9: FIRST THURSDAY OF LENT

JESUS'S DESIRE TO SUFFER FOR US

Oh, how exceedingly tender, loving, and constraining was that declaration of our Blessed Redeemer concerning His coming into the world when He said that He had come to kindle in souls the fire of divine love, and that His only desire was that this holy flame should be enkindled in the hearts of men: *I am come to cast fire upon the earth; and what will I but that it should be kindled?*[35] He continued immediately to say that He was expecting to be baptized with the baptism of His own blood—not, indeed, to wash out His own sins, since He was incapable of sinning, but to wash out our sins, which He had come to satisfy by His sufferings: "The passion of Christ is called baptism, because we are purified in His blood." And therefore our loving Jesus, in order to make us understand how ardent was His desire to die

---

[35]   Luke 12:49.

for us, added, with sweetest expression of His love, that He felt an immense longing for the time of His passion, so great was His desire to suffer for our sake. These are His loving words: *I have a baptism wherewith I am to be baptized; and how am I straitened until it be accomplished?*[36]

O God, the lover of men, what more could You have said or done in order to put me under the necessity of loving You? And what good could my love ever do You, that You chose to die, and so much desired death in order to obtain it? If a servant of mine had only desired to die for me, he would have attracted my love, and can I then live without loving You with all my heart, my king and God, who died for me, and who had such a longing for death in order to acquire to Yourself my love?

Jesus, knowing that His hour was come that He should pass out of the world to the Father, having loved His own, . . . He loved them unto the end.[37] Saint John says that Jesus called the hour of His passion *His* hour because, as a devout commentator writes, this was the time for which our Redeemer had most sighed during His whole life, because by suffering and dying for men, He desired to make them understand the immense love that He bore to them: "That is the hour of the lover, in which He suffers for the object beloved:"[38] because suffering for the beloved is the

---

[36] Luke 12:50.
[37] John 13:1.
[38] *Barrad.* T. iv. l. 2, c. 5.

most fit way of discovering the love of the lover, and of captivating to ourself the love of the beloved.

O my dearest Jesus, in order to show me the great love You bear me, You would not commit the work of my redemption to any other than Yourself. Was my love, then, of such consequence to You that You would suffer so much in order to gain it? Oh, what more could You have done if You had had to gain to Yourself the love of Your divine Father? What more could a servant endure to acquire to himself the affections of his master than what You have suffered in order that You might be loved by me, a vile, ungrateful slave?

MEDITATION 10: FIRST FRIDAY OF LENT

SUFFERING WITH PATIENCE

To speak of patience and suffering is a thing neither practiced nor understood by those who love the world. It is understood and practiced only by souls who love God. "O Lord," said Saint John of the Cross to Jesus Christ, "I ask nothing of You but to suffer and to be despised for Your sake." Saint Teresa frequently exclaimed, "O my Jesus, I would either suffer or die." Saint Mary Magdalene of Pazzi was wont to say, "I would suffer and not die." Thus speak the saints who love God, because a soul can give no surer mark to God of love for Him than voluntarily to suffer to please Him. This is the great proof which Jesus Christ has given of His love to us. As God, He loved us in creating us, in providing us so many blessings, in calling us to enjoy the same glory that He Himself enjoys, but in nothing else has He more fully shown how much He loves us than in becoming man and embracing a painful life and a death full of pangs and ignominies for love of us. And how shall we show our love for Jesus Christ? By leading a life full of pleasures and earthly delights?

Let us not think that God delights in our pains; the Lord is not of so cruel a nature as to be delighted to see us, His creatures, groan and suffer. He is a God of infinite goodness, who desires to see us fully content and happy so that He is full of sweetness, affability, and compassion to all who come to Him.[39] But our unhappy condition, as sinners, and the gratitude we owe to the love of Jesus Christ require that, for His love, we should renounce the delights of this earth and embrace with affection the cross which He gives us to carry during this life, after Him who goes before, bearing a cross far heavier than ours; and all this in order to bring us, after our death, to a blessed life which will never end. God, then, has no desire to see us suffer, but being Himself infinite justice, He cannot leave our faults unpunished so that, in order that they may be punished and yet we may one day attain eternal happiness, He would have us purge away our sins with patience, and thus deserve to be eternally blessed. What can be more beautiful and sweet than this rule of divine Providence, that we see at once justice satisfied and ourselves saved and happy?

All our hopes, then, we must derive from the merits of Jesus Christ, and from Him we must hope for all aid to live holily, and save ourselves; and we cannot doubt that it is His desire to see

---

[39]   Cf. Ps. 85:5.

us holy: *This is the will of God, your sanctification.*[40] But true as this is, we must not neglect to do our part to satisfy God for the injuries we have done to Him, and to attain with our good works to eternal life. This the Apostle expressed when he said, *I fill up that which is wanting of the passion of Christ in my flesh.*[41] Was the passion of Christ, then, not complete, not enough alone to save us? It was most complete in its value and most sufficient to save all men; nevertheless, in order that the merits of the Passion may be applied to us, says Saint Teresa, we must do our part and suffer with patience the crosses which God sends us, that we may be like our head, Jesus Christ, according to what the Apostle writes to the Romans: *Whom He foreknew, them He also predestinated to be conformed to the image of His Son, that He might be the firstborn among many brethren.*[42] Still we must ever remember, as the Angelic Doctor warns us, that all the virtue of our good works, satisfactions, and penances is communicated to them by the satisfaction of Jesus Christ: *The satisfaction of man has its efficacy from the satisfaction of Christ.*[43] And thus we reply to the Protestants, who call our penances injurious to the passion of Jesus Christ, as if it were not sufficient to satisfy for our sins.

---

[40] 1 Thess. 4:3.

[41] Col. 1:24.

[42] Rom. 8:29.

[43] *S. T.*, III, q. 1, a. 2, ad 2.

Meditation II: First Saturday of Lent

Choosing Mortification

We must, then (I repeat), do ourselves violence in order to be saved. But this violence is such (it will be said by someone) that I cannot do it of myself if God does not give it me through His grace. To such a one Saint Ambrose says, "If you look to yourself, you can do nothing, but if you trust in God, strength will be given you." But, in doing this, we must suffer, and it is impossible to avoid it; if we would enter into the glory of the Blessed, says the Scripture, we must, through much tribulation, enter into the kingdom of God.[44] Thus Saint John, beholding the glory of the saints in heaven, heard a voice saying, *These are they who have come out of great tribulation, and have washed their garments, and have made them white in the blood of the Lamb.*[45] It is true that they all attained heaven by being washed in the blood of the Lamb, but they all went there after suffering great tribulation.

---

[44] See Acts 14:21.
[45] Apoc. 7:14.

Be assured, Saint Paul wrote to his disciples, that God is faithful, who will not suffer you to be tempted above what you are able.[46] God has promised to give us sufficient help to conquer every temptation if only we ask Him. *Ask, and it shall be given you; seek, and you shall find.*[47] He cannot, therefore, fail of His promise. It is a fatal error of the heretics to say that God commands things which it is impossible for us to observe. The Council of Trent says: *God does not command impossible things, but when He commands, He bids us do what we can, and seek help for what we cannot do, and He will help us.*[48] Saint Ephrem writes, "If men do not put upon their beasts a greater burden than they can bear, much less does God lay greater temptations upon men than they can endure."[49]

Thomas à Kempis writes, "The cross everywhere awaits you; it is needful for you everywhere to preserve patience, if you would have peace. If you willingly bear the cross, it will bear you to your desired end."[50] In this world, we all of us go about seeking peace—and would find it without suffering, but this is not possible in our present state; we must suffer; the cross awaits us wherever we turn. How, then, can we find peace in the midst of these crosses? By patience, by embracing the cross, which presents itself to us. Saint Teresa says "that he who drags the cross

---

[46]   See 1 Cor. 10:13.

[47]   Matt. 7:7.

[48]   Session 6, chapter 11.

[49]   *De Patientia.*

[50]   De *Imitatione Christi*, Book 2, chapter 12.

along with ill-will feels its weight, however small it is, but he who willingly embraces it, however great it is, does not feel it."

The same Thomas à Kempis says, "Which of the saints is without a cross? The whole life of Christ was a cross and a martyrdom, and you seek for pleasure?" Jesus, innocent, holy, and the Son of God, was willing to suffer through His whole life, and shall we go about seeking pleasures and comforts? To give us an example of patience, He chose a life full of ignominies and pains within and without, and shall we wish to be saved without suffering, or to suffer without patience, which is a double suffering, and without fruit, and with increase of pain? How can we think to be lovers of Jesus Christ if we will not suffer for love of Him who has so much suffered for love of us? How can he glory in being a follower of the Crucified who refuses or receives with ill-will the fruits of the cross, which are sufferings, contempt, poverty, pains, infirmities, and all things that are contrary to our self-love?

Meditation 12: Second Sunday of Lent

Jesus's Desire to Die for Us

So great was the desire of Jesus to suffer for us that in the night preceding His death, He not only went of His own will into the garden, where He knew that the Jews would come and take Him, but, knowing that Judas the traitor was already near at hand with the company of soldiers, He said to His disciples, *Arise, let us go; behold he that will betray Me is at hand.*[51] He would even go Himself to meet them, as if they came to conduct Him, not to the punishment of death, but to the crown of a great kingdom.

O my sweet Savior, You, then, go to meet Your death with such a longing to die, through the desire that You have to be loved by me! And shall I not have a desire to die for You, my God, in order to prove to You the love that I bear You? Yes, my Jesus, who has died for me, I do also desire to die for You. Behold, my blood,

---

[51]   Mark 14:42.

my life, I offer all to You. I am ready to die for You as You will and when You will. Accept this miserable sacrifice which a miserable sinner offers to You, who once offended You, but now loves You more than himself.

Saint Laurence Justinian, in considering this word "I thirst," which Jesus pronounced on the cross when He was expiring, says that this thirst was not a thirst which proceeded from dryness but one that arose from the ardor of the love that Jesus had for us: "This thirst springs from the fever of His love."[52] Because by this word our Redeemer intended to declare to us, more than the thirst of the body, the desire that He had of suffering for us, by showing us His love and the immense desire that He had of being loved by us, by the many sufferings that He endured for us: "This thirst proceeds from the fever of His love." And Saint Thomas says, "By this 'I thirst' is shown the ardent desire for the salvation of the human race."[53]

O God, enamored of souls, is it possible that such an excess of goodness can remain without correspondence on our part? It is said that love must be repaid by love, but by what love can Your love ever be repaid? It would be necessary for another God to die for You in order to compensate for the love that You have borne us in dying for us. And how, then, could You, O my Lord, say that Your delight was to dwell with men[54] if You received

---

[52] *De Tr. Chr. Ag.* c. 19.
[53] *In Joannem,* c. 19, lect. 5, n. 2447.
[54] See Prov. 8:31.

from them nothing but injuries and ill-treatment? Love made You, then, change into delights the sufferings and the insults that You have endured for us. O my Redeemer, most worthy of love, I will no longer resist the stratagems of Your love; I give You from henceforth my whole love. You are and shall be always the only beloved one of my soul. You became man in order that You may have a life to devote to me; I would fain have a thousand lives in order that I may sacrifice them all for You. I love You, O infinite goodness, and I will love You with all my strength. I will do all that lies in my power to please You. You, being innocent, have suffered for me; I a sinner, who have deserved hell, desire to suffer for You as much as You will. O my Jesus, assist, I pray You, by Your merits, this desire which You Yourself give me. O infinite God, I believe in You, I hope in You, I love You. Mary, my Mother, intercede for me. Amen.

MEDITATION 13: SECOND MONDAY OF LENT

THE SACRAMENT OF LOVE

Jesus, knowing that His hour was come that He should pass out of this world to the Father, having loved His own who were in the world, He loved them to the end.[55] Our most loving Redeemer, on the last night of His life, knowing that the much longed-for time had arrived on which He should die for the love of man, had not the heart to leave us alone in this valley of tears. But in order that He might not be separated from us even by death, He would leave us His whole self as food in the Sacrament of the Altar, giving us to understand by this that, having given us this gift of infinite worth, He could give us nothing further to prove to us His love: *He loved them unto the end.* Cornelius à Lapide, with Saint Chrysostom and Theophylact, interprets the words "unto the end" according to the Greek text, and writes thus: "He loved them with an excessive and supreme love." Jesus

---

[55] John 13:1.

in this sacrament made His last effort of love towards men, as
the Abbot Guerric says: "He poured out the whole power of
His love upon His friends."[56]

This was still better expressed by the holy Council of Trent,
which, in speaking of the Sacrament of the Altar, says that our
Blessed Savior "poured out of Himself in it, as it were, all the
riches of His love towards us."[57]

The angelic Saint Thomas was therefore right in calling this
sacrament "a sacrament of love, and a token of the greatest love
that God could give us." And Saint Bernard called it "the love of
loves." And Saint Mary Magdalene of Pazzi said that a soul, after
having communicated, might say, "It is consummated"; that is to
say, My God, having given Himself to me in this Holy Communion, has nothing more to give me. This saint, one day asked one
of her novices what she had been thinking of after Communion;
she answered, "Of the *love of Jesus.*" "Yes," replied the saint, "when
we think of this love, we cannot pass on to other thoughts, but
must stop upon love."

O Savior of the world, what do You expect from men that
You have been induced even to give them Yourself in food? And
what can there be left to You to give us after this sacrament in
order to oblige us to love You? Ah, my most loving God, enlighten me that I may know what an excess of goodness this
has been of Yours to reduce Yourself unto becoming my food in

---

56   *Sermo de Ascensione Domini.*
57   Session 13, chapter 2.

Holy Communion! If You have, therefore, given Yourself entirely to me, it is just that I also should give myself wholly to You. Yes, my Jesus, I give myself entirely to You. I love You above every good, and I desire to receive You in order to love You more. Come, therefore, and come often, into my soul, and make it entirely Yours. Oh that I could truly say to You, as the loving Saint Philip Neri said to You when he received You in the Viaticum, "Behold my love, behold my love; give me my love."

MEDITATION 14: SECOND TUESDAY OF LENT

JESUS ANNIHILATES HIMSELF IN THE HOLY EUCHARIST

*H*e *that eats My flesh, and drinks My blood, abides in Me, and I in him.*[58] Saint Denis the Areopagite says that love always tends towards union with the object beloved. And because food becomes one thing with him who eats it, therefore Our Lord would reduce Himself to food in order that, receiving Him in Holy Communion, we might become of one substance with Him: *Take and eat,* said Jesus; *this is My body.*[59] As if He had said, remarks Saint John Chrysostom, "Eat Me, that the highest union may take place."[60] O man, feed yourself on Me in order that you and I may become one substance. In the same way, says Saint Cyril of Alexandria, as two pieces of

---

58   John 6:57.
59   Matt. 26:26.
60   *In I ad Timotheum,* homilia 15.

melted wax unite together, so a soul that communicates is so thoroughly united to Jesus that Jesus remains in it, and it in Jesus. O my beloved Redeemer, exclaims, therefore, Saint Laurence Justinian, how could You ever come to love us so much that You would unite Yourself to us in such a way that Your heart and ours should become but one heart? "Oh, how admirable is Your love, O Lord Jesus, who would incorporate us in such a manner with Your body that we should have but one heart with You."[61]

Well did Saint Francis de Sales say, in speaking of Holy Communion: "In no action does our Savior show Himself more loving or more tender than in this one, in which, as it were, He annihilates Himself and reduces Himself to food in order to penetrate our souls and unite Himself to the hearts of His faithful ones." So that, says Saint John Chrysostom, "To that Lord on whom the angels even dare not fix their eyes, to Him we unite ourselves, and we are made one body, one flesh." "But what shepherd," adds the saint, "feeds the sheep with his own blood? Even mothers give their children to nurses to feed them, but Jesus in the Blessed Sacrament feeds us with His own blood and unites us to Himself. What shepherd feeds his sheep with his own blood? And why do I say shepherd? There are many mothers who give their children to others to nurse, but this He has not done, but feeds us with His own blood."[62] In short, says the saint,

---

[61]   *De Inc. div. cm. c. 5.*
[62]   *Ad populum Antiochenum* homilia, 60.

because He loves us so ardently, He chose to make Himself one with us by becoming our food. "He mixed Himself with us, that we might be one; this they do whose love is ardent."[63]

O infinite love, worthy of infinite love, when shall I love You, my Jesus, as You have loved me? O divine food, sacrament of love, when will You draw me entirely to Yourself? You have nothing left to do in order to make Yourself loved by me. I am constantly intending to begin to love You; I constantly promise You to do so, but I never begin. I will from this day begin to love You in earnest. Oh, enable me to do so. Enlighten me, inflame me, detach me from earth, and permit me not any longer to resist so many enticements of Your love. I love You with my whole heart, and I will therefore leave everything in order to please You, my life, my love, my all. I will constantly unite myself to You in this Holy Sacrament in order to detach myself from everything and to love You only, my God. I hope, through Your gracious assistance, to be enabled to do so.

---

[63]   *Ad populum Antiochenum* homilia, 61.

MEDITATION 15: SECOND
WEDNESDAY OF LENT

WHY DOES GOD LOVE US?

Saint Bernard says that God loves us for no other reason than that He may be loved by us: "God only loved that He might be loved."[64] And therefore our Savior protested that He had come upon earth in order to make Himself loved: *I am come to send a fire upon the earth.*[65] And oh, what flames of holy love does Jesus kindle in souls in this most divine Sacrament! The Venerable Father Francis Olimpio, a Theatine, said that nothing was so fit to excite our hearts to love the sovereign good as the most Holy Communion. Hesychius called Jesus in the Sacrament a "divine fire." And Saint Catherine of Siena, one day perceiving, in the hands of a priest, Jesus in the Sacrament under the appearance of a furnace of love, was full of astonishment that the whole world was not consumed by the fire. The Abbot Rupert

---

[64] *In Canticum Canticorum*, sermo 83.
[65] Luke 12:49.

and Saint Gregory of Nyssa said that the altar itself was the wine cellar where the espoused soul is inebriated with the love of her Lord, so much so, that, forgetful of earth, she burns and languishes with holy love: *The king brought me*, says the spouse in the Canticles, *into the cellar of wine; he set in order charity in me. Stay me up with flowers, compass me about with apples: because I languish with love.*[66]

O love of my soul, most Holy Sacrament; oh that I could always remember You, to forget everything else, and that I could love You alone without interruption and without reserve! Ah, my Jesus, You have knocked so frequently at the door of my heart that You have at last, I hope, entered therein. But since You have entered there, drive away, I pray You, all its affections that do not tend towards Yourself. Possess Yourself so entirely of me that I may be able with truth to say to You from this day forth, with the Prophet, *What have I in heaven? And besides You what do I desire on earth? . . . The God of my heart, . . . and my portion forever.*[67] Yes, O my God, what else do I desire but You upon earth or in heaven? You alone are and shall always be the only Lord of my heart and my will, and You alone shall be all my portion, all my riches, in this life and in the next.

Go, said the Prophet Isaiah—go, publish everywhere the loving inventions of our God, in order to make Himself loved of men: *You shall draw waters with joy out of the Savior's fountains;*

---

[66]   Cant. 2:4–5.
[67]   Ps. 72:25–26.

and you shall say in that day, Praise the Lord, and call upon His name, make His inventions known among the people.[68] And what inventions has not the love of Jesus made in order to make Himself loved by us? Even on the cross He has opened in His wounds so many fountains of grace that to receive them it is sufficient to ask for them in faith. And, not satisfied with this, He has given us His whole self in the Most Holy Sacrament.

---

[68]   Is. 12:3–4.

MEDITATION 16: SECOND THURSDAY OF LENT

JESUS'S FEAR OF DEATH

Behold, our most loving Savior, having come to the Garden of Gethsemane, did of His own accord make a beginning of His bitter passion by giving full liberty to the passions of fear, of weariness, and of sorrow to come and afflict Him with all their torments: *He began to fear and to be heavy,*[69] *to grow sorrowful, and to be sad.*[70]

He began, then, first to feel a great fear of death and of the sufferings He would have soon to endure. *He began to fear,* but how? Was it not He Himself that had offered Himself spontaneously to endure all these torments? *He was offered because He willed it.*[71] Was it not He who had so much desired this hour of His passion, and who had said shortly before, *With desire have I*

---

69 Mark 14:33.
70 Matt. 26:37.
71 Is. 53:7.

desired to eat this pasch with you?[72] And yet how is it that He was
seized with such a fear of death, that He even prayed His Father
to deliver Him from it? *My Father, if it be possible, let this chalice
pass from Me.*[73] The Venerable Bede answers this, and says, "He
prays that the chalice may pass from Him in order to show that
He was truly man."[74] He, our loving Savior, chose indeed to die
for us in order to prove to us by His death the love that He bore
us, but in order that men might not suppose that He had assumed an imaginary body (as some heretics have blasphemously
asserted), or that by virtue of His divinity He had died without
suffering any pain, He therefore made this prayer to His heavenly
Father, not indeed with a view to being heard, but to give us to
understand that He died as man, and afflicted with a great fear of
death and of the sufferings which should accompany His death.

O most amiable Jesus! You would, then, take upon You our
fearfulness in order to give us Your courage in suffering the trials
of this life. Oh, be You forever blessed for Your great mercy and
love! Oh, may all our hearts love You as much as You desire, and
as much as You deserve!

He began to be heavy. He began to feel a great weariness on
account of the torments that were prepared for Him. When
one is weary, even pleasures are painful. Oh, what anguish united to this weariness must Jesus Christ have felt at the horrible

---

[72]   Luke 22:15.
[73]   Matt. 26:39.
[74]   *In Marcum* 14.

representation which then came before His mind, of all the
torments, both exterior and interior, which, during the short
remainder of His life, were so cruelly to afflict His body and
His blessed soul! Then did all the sufferings He was to endure
pass distinctly before His eyes, as well as all the insults that
He should endure from the Jews and from the Romans; all
the injustice of which the judges of His cause would be guilty
towards Him; and, above all, He had before Him the vision
of that death of desolation which He should have to endure,
forsaken by all, by men and by God, in the midst of a sea of
sufferings and contempt. And this it was that caused Him so
heavy grief that He was obliged to pray for consolation to His
eternal Father. O my Jesus! I compassionate You, I thank You,
and I love You.

MEDITATION 17: SECOND FRIDAY OF LENT

JESUS'S SORROW

He began to grow sorrowful and to be sad.[75] Together with this fear and weariness, Jesus began to feel a great melancholy and affliction of soul. But, my Lord, are You not He who gave to Your martyrs such a delight in suffering that they even despised their torments and death? Saint Augustine[76] said of Saint Vincent that he spoke with such joy during his martyrdom that it seemed as if it were not the same person that suffered and that spoke. It is related of Saint Laurence that while he was burning on the gridiron, such was the consolation he enjoyed in his soul that he defied the tyrant, saying, "Turn, and eat." How, then, my Jesus, did You, who gave such great joy to Your servants in dying, choose for Yourself such extreme sorrowfulness in Your death?

O delight of paradise, You rejoice heaven and earth with Your gladness; why, then, do I behold You so afflicted and sorrowful?

---

[75]   Matt. 26:37.

[76]   *Serm. 275, E. B.*

Why do I hear You say that the sorrow that afflicts You is enough to take away Your life? *My soul is sorrowful even unto death.*[77] O my Redeemer, why is this? Ah, I understand it all. It was less the thought of Your sufferings in Your bitter passion than of the sins of men that afflicted You, and among these, alas, were my sins, which caused You this great dread of death.

He, the Eternal Word, as much as He loved His Father, so much did He hate sin, of which He well knew the malice; wherefore, in order to deliver the world from sin, and that He might no longer behold His beloved Father offended, He had come upon earth, and had made Himself man, and had undertaken to suffer so painful a death and Passion. But when He saw that, notwithstanding all His sufferings, there would yet be so many sins committed in the world, His sorrow for this, says Saint Thomas, exceeded the sorrow that any penitent has ever felt for his own sins: "It surpassed the sorrow of all contrite souls,"[78] and, indeed, it surpassed every sorrow that ever could afflict a human heart. The reason is that all the sorrows that men feel are always mixed with some relief, but the sorrow of Jesus was pure sorrow without any relief: "He suffered pure pain without any admixture of consolation."[79]

Oh, if I loved You, my Jesus—if I loved You, the consideration of all that You have suffered for me would render all sufferings, all

---

[77] Mark 14:34.
[78] *S. T.*, III, q. 46, a. 6, ad 4.
[79] Vincent Contenson, *Theologia Mentis et Cordis*, I. 10, d. 4, c. 1, sp. 1.

contempt, and all vexations sweet to me. Oh, grant me, I beseech You, Your love in order that I may endure with pleasure, or at least with patience, the little You give me to suffer. Oh, let me not die so ungrateful to all Your loving-kindnesses. I desire, in all the tribulations that shall happen to me, to say constantly, My Jesus, I embrace this trial for Your love; I will suffer it in order to please You.

MEDITATION 18: SECOND SATURDAY OF LENT

THE MALICE OF SIN

We read in history that several penitents being enlightened by divine light to see the malice of their sins have died of pure sorrow for them. Oh, what torment, then, must not the heart of Jesus endure at the sight of all the sins of the world, of all the blasphemies, sacrileges, acts of impurity, and all the other crimes which should be committed by men after His death, every one of which, like a wild beast, tore His heart separately by its own malice? Wherefore our afflicted Lord, during His agony in the garden, exclaimed, "Is this, therefore, O men, the reward that you render Me for My immeasurable love? Oh, if I could only see that, grateful for My affection, you gave up sin and began to love Me, with what delight should I not hasten to die for you! But to behold, after all My sufferings, so many sins; after so much love, such ingratitude;—this is what afflicts Me the most, makes Me sorrowful even unto death, and makes Me sweat pure blood": *And His sweat became as drops of blood trickling down upon the ground.*[80] So that, according to the Evangelist, this bloody sweat was so copious that it first bathed all the vestments of our Blessed Redeemer, and then came forth in quantity and bathed the ground.

Ah, my loving Jesus, I do not behold in this garden either scourges or thorns or nails that pierce You; how, then, is it that I see You all bathed in blood from Your head to Your feet? Alas, my sins were the cruel press which, by dint of affliction and sorrow, drew so much blood from Your heart. I was, then, one of Your most cruel executioners, who contributed the most to crucify You with my sins. It is certain that, if I had sinned less, You, my Jesus, would have suffered less. As much pleasure, therefore, as I have taken in offending You, so much the more did I increase the sorrow of Your heart, already full of anguish. How, then, does not this thought make me die of grief when I see that I have repaid the love You have shown me in Your passion by adding to Your sorrow and suffering? I, then, have tormented this heart, so loving and so worthy of love, which has shown so much love to me. My Lord, since I have now no other means left of consoling You than to weep over my offenses towards You, I will now, my Jesus, sorrow for them and lament over them with my whole heart. Oh, give me, I pray You, so great sorrow for them as may make me to my last breath weep over the displeasure I have caused You, my God, my Love, my All.

---

[80]   Luke 22:44.

O my afflicted Lord, make me share in that sorrow which You then had for my sins. I abhor them at this present moment, and I unite this my hatred to the horror that You felt for them in the garden. O my Savior, look not upon my sins, for hell itself would not be sufficient to expiate them, but look upon the sufferings that You have endured for me! O love of my Jesus, You are my love and my hope. O my Lord, I love You with my whole soul, and will always love You.

MEDITATION 19: THIRD SUNDAY OF LENT

THE IGNOMINIES OF CHRIST CRUCIFIED

The greatest ignominies that Jesus Christ suffered were those which were offered to Him in His passion. In the first place, He then bore to see Himself abandoned by His beloved disciples; one of them betrayed Him, another denied Him, and when He was captured in the garden, all fled and abandoned Him: *Then His disciples leaving Him, all fled away.*[81] Afterwards the Jews presented Him to Pilate as a malefactor who deserved to be crucified. *If,* said they, *He were not a malefactor, we would not have delivered Him up to you.*[82] Herod treated Him as a fool: *Herod,* says Saint Luke, *with his army, set Him at nought and mocked Him, putting on Him a white garment.*[83]

---

[81]   Mark 14:50.

[82]   John 18:30.

[83]   Luke 23:11.

Barabbas, a robber and murderer, was preferred before Him. When Pilate gave the Jews the choice of rescuing Jesus Christ or Barabbas from death, they exclaimed, *Not this man, but Barabbas*.[84] He was chastised with the lash, a punishment inflicted only on slaves: *Then, therefore, says John, Pilate took Jesus and scourged Him*.[85] He was treated as a mock king; for after having through mockery crowned Him with thorns, they saluted Him as king and spat in His face: *They mocked Him, saying, Hail, King of the Jews. And spitting upon Him, they took the reed, and struck His head*.[86] He was afterwards, as Isaiah had foretold, condemned to die between two malefactors: *He was reputed with the wicked*.[87]

Finally, He died on the cross: that is the most opprobrious death which was then inflicted on malefactors, for the man whom the Jews condemned to the death of the cross was, as we read in Deuteronomy,[88] said to be an object of malediction to God and man. Hence, Saint Paul has said, *Being made a curse for us* (that is, a mere curse), *for it is written, Cursed is every one that hangs on a tree*.[89] Our Redeemer, says the same Apostle, renouncing the life of splendor and happiness which He might enjoy on this earth, chose for Himself a life full of tribulations

---

[84]   John 18:40.
[85]   John 19:1.
[86]   Matt. 27:29–30.
[87]   Is. 53:12.
[88]   See Deut. 21:23.
[89]   Gal. 3:13.

and a death accompanied with so much shame: *Who, having joy set before Him, endured the cross, despising the shame.*[90]

Thus in Jesus Christ was fulfilled the prediction of Jeremiah, that He should live and die saturated with opprobrium. *He shall give His cheek to him that strikes Him, He shall be filled with reproaches.*[91] Hence Saint Bernard exclaims, "O grandeur! O abasement!"[92] Behold the Lord, who is exalted above all, become the most contemptible of all. The holy Doctor then concludes that all this proceeded from the love which Jesus Christ bore us.[93]

O my Jesus, save me; do not permit me, after being redeemed by You with so much pain and so much love, to lose my soul and go to hell, there to hate and curse the very love which You have borne me. This hell I have indeed so often deserved; for, though You could do nothing more than You have done to oblige me to love You, I have done everything in my power to compel You to chastise me. But since, in Your goodness, You have waited for me, and even still continue to ask me to love You, I wish to love You: I wish henceforth to love You with my whole heart and without reserve. Give me strength to make this wish effective. O Mary, Mother of God, assist me by your prayers.

---

[90]   Heb. 12:2.
[91]   Lam. 3:30.
[92]   *Sermo de Passione Domini.*
[93]   *In Canticum Canticorum,* sermo 64.

JESUS IS SPAT UPON

Then they spat in His face and buffeted Him.[94] After having proclaimed Him guilty of death, as a man already given over to punishment and declared infamous, the rabble set themselves to ill-treat Him all the night through with blows, and buffets, and kicks, with plucking out His beard, and even spitting in His face, by mocking Him as a false prophet and saying, *Prophesy to us, O Christ, who it is that struck You.*[95] All this our Redeemer foretold by Isaiah: *I have given My body to the strikers, and My cheeks to them that plucked them: I have not turned away My face from them that rebuked Me and spit upon Me.*[96] The devout Tauler[97] relates that it is an opinion of Saint Jerome that all the pains and infirmities which Jesus suffered on that night will be made

---

[94] Matt. 26:67.

[95] Matt. 26:68.

[96] Is. 50:6.

[97] *De Vita et Passione Salvatoris,* chapter 17.

known only on the day of the last judgment. Saint Augustine, speaking of the ignominies suffered by Jesus Christ, says, "If this medicine cannot cure our pride, I know not what can."[98] Ah, my Jesus, how is it that You are so humble and I so proud? O Lord, give me light, make me know who You are, and who I am.

Then they spat in His face. "Spat!" O God, what greater affront can there be than to be defiled by spitting? "To be spit upon is to suffer the extreme of insult,"[99] says Origen. Where are we wont to spit except in the most filthy place? And did You, my Jesus, suffer Yourself to be spit upon in the face? Behold how these wretches outrage You with blows and kicks, insult You, spit on Your face, do with You just what they will, and do You not threaten nor reprove them? *When He was reviled, He reviled not; when He suffered, He threatened not; but delivered Himself to him that judged Him unjustly.*[100] No, but like an innocent lamb, humble and meek, You suffered all without so much as complaining, offering all to the Father to obtain the pardon of our sins: *Like a lamb before the shearer, He shall be dumb, and shall not open His mouth.*[101]

Saint Gertrude one day, when meditating on the injuries done to Jesus in His passion, began to praise and bless Him; this was so pleasing to Our Lord that He lovingly thanked her.

---

[98]   *Serm. 77, E. B.*
[99]   *In Matthaeum,* tractus 35.
[100]   1 Ptr. 2:23.
[101]   Is. 53:7.

Ah, my reviled Lord, You are the King of heaven, the Son of the Most High; You surely deserved not to be ill-treated and despised, but to be adored and loved by all creatures. I adore You, I bless You, I thank You, I love You with all my heart. I repent of having offended You. Help me, have pity upon me.

THE REPROACH OF MEN

Presently we will speak of the other reproaches which Jesus Christ endured, until He finally died on the cross: *He endured the cross, despising the shame.*[102] In the meanwhile let us consider how truly in our Redeemer was fulfilled what the Psalmist had foretold, that in His passion He should become the reproach of men, and the outcast of the people: *But I am a worm, and no man; the reproach of men, and the outcast of the people,*[103] even to a death of ignominy, suffered at the hands of the executioner on a cross, as a malefactor between two malefactors: *And He was reputed with the wicked.*[104]

O Lord, the Most High, exclaims Saint Bernard, become the lowest among men! O lofty one become vile! O glory of angels

---

[102]   Heb. 12:2.
[103]   Ps. 21.7.
[104]   Is. 53:12.

become the reproach of men! "O lowest and highest! O humble and sublime! O reproach of men and glory of angels!"[105]

"O grace, O strength of the love of God!" continues Saint Bernard. Thus did the Lord Most High over all become the most lightly esteemed of all. "O grace, O power of love, did the highest of all thus become the lowest of all?" And who was it (adds the saint) that did this? "Who hath done this? Love."[106] All this has the love which God bears towards men done, to prove how He loves us, and to teach us by His example how to suffer with peace contempt and injuries: *Christ suffered for us* (writes Saint Peter), *leaving you an example, that you may follow His steps.*[107] Saint Eleazar, when asked by his wife how he came to endure with such peace the great injuries that were done him, answered, "I turn to look on Jesus enduring contempt and say that my affronts are as nothing in respect to those which He my God was willing to bear for me."

Ah, my Jesus, and how is it that, at the sight of a God thus dishonored for love of me, I know not how to suffer the least contempt for love of You? A sinner, and proud! And whence, my Lord, can come this pride? I pray You by the merits of the contempt You suffered, give me grace to suffer with patience and gladness all affronts and injuries. From this day forth I propose by Your help nevermore to resent them, but to receive with joy

---

[105] *Sermo de Passione Domini.*
[106] *In Canticum Canticorum,* sermo 64.
[107] 1 Ptr. 2:21.

all the reproaches that shall be offered me. Truly have I deserved greater contempt for having despised Your divine majesty, and deserved the contempt of hell. Exceeding sweet and pleasant to me have You rendered affronts, my beloved Redeemer, by having embraced so great contempt for love of me. Henceforth I propose, in order to please You, to benefit as much as possible whoever despises me; at least to speak well of and pray for him. And even now I pray You to heap Your graces upon all those from whom I have received any injury. I love You, O infinite good, and will ever love You as much as I can. Amen.

MEDITATION 22: THIRD WEDNESDAY OF LENT

THE CRUELTY OF THE SCOURGING

Saint Bonaventure sorrowfully exclaims, "The royal blood is flowing; bruise is superadded to bruise, and gash to gash."[108] That divine blood was already issuing from every pore; that sacred body was already become but one perfect wound; yet those infuriated brutes did not forbear to add blow to blow, as the Prophet had foretold: *And they have added to the grief of my wounds,*[109] so that the thongs not only made the whole body one wound but even bore away pieces of it into the air, until at length the gashes in that sacred flesh were such that the bones might have been counted: "The flesh was so torn away, that the bones could be numbered."[110] Cornelius à Lapide says that in

---

[108] *Med. vit. Chr. c.* 76.
[109] Ps. 68:27.
[110] Vincent Contenson, *Theologia Mentis et Cordis,* l. 10, d. 4, c. 1, sp. 1.

this torment Jesus Christ ought, naturally speaking, to have died, but He willed, by His divine power, to keep Himself in life in order to suffer yet greater pains for love of us. And Saint Laurence Justinian had observed the same thing before: "He evidently ought to have died. Yet He reserved Himself unto life, it being His will to endure heavier sufferings."[111]

Ah, my most loving Lord, You are worthy of an infinite love; You have suffered so much in order that I might love You. Oh, never permit me, instead of loving You, to offend or displease You more! Oh, what place in hell should there not be set apart for me if, after having known the love that You have borne towards such a wretch, I should damn myself, despising a God who had suffered scorn, smitings, and scourgings for me and who had, moreover, after my having so often offended Him, so mercifully pardoned me! Ah, my Jesus, let it not, oh, let it not be thus! O my God! How would the love and the patience which You have shown towards me be there for me in hell, another hell even yet more full of torments!

Cruel in excess to our Redeemer was this torture of His scourging in the first place, because of the great number of those by whom it was inflicted, who, as was revealed to Saint Mary Magdalene of Pazzi, were not fewer than sixty. And these, at the instigation of the devils, and even more so of the priests, who were afraid lest Pilate should, after this punishment, be minded to release the Lord, as he had already protested to them, saying, *I*

---

[111] *De Tr. Chr. Ag. c.* 14.

will therefore scourge Him, and let Him go,[112] aimed at taking away His life by means of this scourging. Again, all theologians agree with Saint Bonaventure that, for this purpose, the sharpest implements were selected so that, as Saint Anselm declares, every stroke produced a wound and that the number of the strokes amounted to several thousand, the flagellation being administered, as Father Crasset says, not after the manner of the Jews, for whom the Lord had forbidden that the number of strokes should ever exceed forty—*Yet so, that they exceed not the number of forty; lest your brother depart shamefully torn*[113]—but after the manner of the Romans, with whom there was no measure.

---

[112] Luke 23:22.

[113] Deut. 25:3.

THE PULPIT OF THE CROSS

Your eyes shall behold your teacher.[114] It was promised to men that with their own eyes they should see their divine Master. The whole life of Jesus was one continuous example and school of perfection, but never did He better inculcate His own most excellent virtues than from the pulpit of His cross. There what an admirable instruction does He give us on patience, more especially in time of infirmity; for with what constancy does Jesus upon the cross endure with most perfect patience the pains of His most bitter death! There, by His own example, He teaches us an exact obedience to the divine precepts, a perfect resignation to God's will, and, above all, He teaches us how we ought to love. Father Paul Segneri, the younger, wrote to one of his penitents that she ought to keep these words written at the foot of the crucifix: "See what it is to love." It seems as though our

---

[114] Is. 30:20.

Redeemer from the cross said to us all, "See what it is to love," whenever, in order to avoid something that is troublesome, we abandon works that are pleasing in His sight, or at times even go so far as to renounce His grace and His love. He has loved us even unto death and came not down from the cross till after having left His life thereon.

Ah, my Jesus, You have loved me, even unto dying for me, and I too wish to love You even unto dying for You. How often have I offended and betrayed You in time past! O my Lord, revenge Yourself upon me, but let it be the revenge of pity and love. Bestow upon me such a sorrow for my sins as may make me live in continual grief and affliction through pain at having offended You. I protest my willingness to suffer every evil for the time to come rather than displease You. And what greater evil could befall me than that of displeasing You, my God, my Redeemer, my hope, my treasure, my all.

And I, if I be lifted up from the earth, will draw all things to Myself. But this He said, signifying what death He should die.[115] Jesus Christ said that when He should have been lifted up upon the cross, He would, by His merits, by His example, and by the power of His love, have drawn towards Himself the affection of all souls: "He drew all the nations of the world to His love, by the merit of His blood, by His example, and by His love." Such is the commentary of Cornelius à Lapide. Saint Peter Damian tells us the same: "The Lord, as soon as He was suspended upon the

---

[115] John 12:32–33.

cross, drew all men to Himself through a loving desire."[116] And who is there, Cornelius goes on to say, that will not love Jesus, who dies for love of us? "For who will not reciprocate the love of Christ, who dies out of love for us?" Behold, O redeemed souls (as Holy Church exhorts us), behold your Redeemer upon that cross, where His whole form breathes love and invites you to love Him: His head bent downwards to give us the kiss of peace, His arms stretched out to embrace us, His heart open to love us: "His whole figure" (as Saint Augustine says) "breathes love and challenges us to love Him in return: His head bent downwards to kiss us, His hands stretched out to embrace us, His bosom open to love us."[117]

Ah, my Jesus, You have loved me, even unto dying for me, and I, too, wish to love You even unto dying for You. How often have I offended and betrayed You in time past! O my Lord, revenge Yourself upon me, but let it be the revenge of pity and love.

---

[116]   *Sermo de Inventione Crucis.*
[117]   *Off. Dol. B. V. resp.* 1.

MEDITATION 24: THIRD FRIDAY OF LENT

THE THIRST OF JESUS

Jesus, drawing nigh unto death, said, "*Sitio,*" I thirst.[118] Tell me, Lord, says Leo of Ostia, for what do You thirst? You make no mention of those immense pains which You suffered upon the cross, but You complain only of thirst: "Lord, what do You thirst for? You are silent about the cross and cry out about the thirst."[119] "My thirst is for your salvation," is the reply which Saint Augustine makes for Him. O soul, says Jesus, this thirst of Mine is nothing but the desire which I have for your salvation. He, the loving Redeemer, with extreme ardor, desires our souls, and therefore He panted to give Himself wholly to us by His death. This was His thirst, wrote Saint Laurence Justinian: "He thirsted for us, and desired to give Himself to us."[120] Saint Basil of Seleucia says, moreover, that Jesus Christ, in saying that He thirsted,

---

118 John 19:28.
119 *Sermo de Passione Domini.*
120 *De Tr. Chr. Ag. c. 19.*

would give us to understand that He, for the love which He bore us, was dying with the desire of suffering for us even more than what He had suffered: "O that desire, greater than the Passion!"

O most lovely God! Because You love us, You desire that we should desire You: "God thirsts to be thirsted for,"[121] as Saint Gregory teaches us. Ah, my Lord, You thirst for me, a most vile worm as I am. And shall I not thirst for You, my infinite God? Oh, by the merits of this thirst endured upon the cross, give me a great thirst to love You and to please You in all things. You have promised to grant us whatever we seek from You: *Ask, and you shall receive.*[122] I ask of You but this one gift—the gift of loving You. I am, indeed, unworthy of it, but in this has to be the glory of Your blood—the turning of a heart into a great lover of You, which has, at one time, so greatly despised You; to make a perfect flame of charity of a sinner who is altogether full of mire and of sins. Much more than this have You done in dying for me. Would that I could love You, O Lord infinitely good, as much as You deserve! I delight in the love which is borne You by the souls that are enamored of You, and still more in the love You bear towards Yourself. With this I unite my own wretched love. I love You, O Eternal God; I love You, O infinite loveliness. Make me ever to increase in Your love, reiterating to You frequent acts of love and studying to please You in everything, without intermission and without reserve. Make me, wretched and insignificant as I may be, make me at least to be all Your own.

---

[121] *Tetr. Sent.* 37.
[122] John 16:24.

MEDITATION 25: THIRD SATURDAY OF LENT

THE INSULTS OFFERED TO JESUS CHRIST ON THE CROSS

Behold also, that, at the very time when He was thus in agonies upon the cross, and was drawing near to death, all they who stood near Him—priests, scribes, elders, and soldiers—wearied themselves in adding to His pangs with insults and mockeries. Saint Matthew writes, *They that passed by blasphemed Him, wagging their heads.*[123] This was already prophesied by David, when he wrote, in the person of Christ, *All they that saw Me reviled Me, they spoke with their lips, and wagged their head.*[124]

They who passed before Him said, *Vah, You that destroy the temple of God, and in three days rebuild it, save Your own self; if You be the Son of God, come down from the cross.*[125] You have

---

[123]   Matt. 27:39.

[124]   Ps. 21:8.

[125]   Matt. 27:40.

boasted, they said, that You would destroy the temple, and rebuild it in three days. Yet Jesus had not said that He could destroy the material temple and raise it again in three days, but He
had said: *Destroy this temple, and in three days I will raise it up
again.*[126] With these words He indeed intended to express His
own power, but He really (as Euthymius and others explain it)
spoke allegorically, foretelling that, through the act of the Jews,
His soul would be one day separated from His body, but that in
three days it would rise again.

They said, *Save Yourself.* O ungrateful men! If this great Son
of God, when He was made man, had chosen to save Himself,
He would not voluntarily have chosen death.

If You are the Son of God, come down from the cross;[127] yet,
if Jesus had come down, He would not have accomplished our
redemption by His death; we could not have been delivered
from eternal death. "He would not come down," says Saint Ambrose, "lest when He came down, I should die."[128] Theophylact
writes that they who said this spoke by the instigation of the
devil, who sought to hinder the salvation which was about to
be accomplished by Jesus by means of the cross.[129] And then he
adds that the Lord would not have mounted the cross if He had
been willing to come down from it without accomplishing our
redemption. Also, Saint John Chrysostom says that the Jews

---

[126] John 2:19.
[127] Matt. 27:40.
[128] *In Lucam*, chapter 23.
[129] See *In Marcum*, chapter 15.

uttered this insult in order that Jesus might die insulted as an impostor in the sight of all men, and be proved unable to deliver Himself from the cross, after He had boasted that He was the Son of God.[130]

Saint John Chrysostom also remarks that the Jews ignorantly said, *If You be the Son of God, come down from the cross*; for if Jesus had come down from the cross before He had died, He would not have been that Son of God who was promised, and who was to save us by His death. On this account, says the saint, He did not come down from the cross until He was dead, because He had come for the very purpose of giving His life for our salvation.[131] Saint Athanasius makes the same remark, saying that our Redeemer chose to be known as the true Son of God, not by coming down from the cross, but by continuing upon it till He was dead.[132] And thus it was foretold by the prophets that our Redeemer must be crucified and die, as Saint Paul wrote, *Christ has redeemed us from the curse of the law, being made a curse for us, for it is written: Cursed is every one who hangs on a tree.*[133]

---

130   See *In Matthaeum*, homilia 88.
131   See *De Cruce et Latrone*, homilia 2.
132   See *Sermo de Passione et Cruce*.
133   Gal. 3:13.

MEDITATION 26: FOURTH SUNDAY OF LENT

THE COUNCIL OF
THE JEWS AND THE
TREACHERY OF JUDAS

*T*he chief priests, therefore, and the Pharisees gathered a council and said: What do we, for this man does many miracles?[134] Behold, at the very time that Jesus Christ was employed in working miracles for the benefit of all, the first personages of the city assembled to plan the death of the author of life. Behold what the impious Caiaphas said: *It is expedient for you that one man should die for the people, and that the whole nation perish not.*[135] From that day, says Saint John, they sought a means of putting Jesus to death.

---

[134] John 11:47.
[135] John 11:50.

Ah, Jews, fear not; this your Redeemer does not fly away; no, He has come on earth to die, and by His death to deliver you and all men from eternal death!

But behold, Judas presents himself to the high priests and says: *What will you give me, and I will deliver Him unto you?*[136] Oh, how great was the joy with which the Jews exulted through the hatred that they bore to Jesus Christ when they saw that one of His own disciples offered to betray Him and to deliver Him into their hands!

Let us here consider the exultation of hell when a soul that has served Jesus Christ for several years betrays Him for a miserable good or a vile pleasure. But, O Judas, since you wish to sell your God, at least demand the price which He is worth. He is an infinite good, and is therefore worth an infinite price. But you conclude the sale for thirty pieces of silver: *But they appointed him thirty pieces of silver.*[137] Ah, my unhappy soul, leave Judas, and turn your thoughts on yourself. Tell me for what price have you so often sold the grace of God to the devil?

Ah, my Jesus, I am ashamed to appear before You when I think of the injuries I have done You. How often have I turned my back upon You, and preferred to You some temporal interest, the indulgence of caprice, or a momentary and vile pleasure? I knew that by such a sin I should lose Your friendship, and I have voluntarily exchanged it for nothing. Oh that I had been dead

---

[136]   Matt. 26:15.
[137]   Matt. 26:15.

rather than have offered You so great an outrage! My Jesus, I repent with my whole heart; I would wish to die of sorrow for it.

Let us here consider the benignity of Jesus Christ, who, though He knew the appointment which Judas had made, did not banish him from His presence when He saw him, nor look at him with an unfriendly eye, but admitted him into His society, and even to His table, and reminded him of his treachery, for the sole purpose of making him enter into himself. When He saw him obstinate, He even prostrated Himself before him and washed his feet in order to soften his heart.

Ah, my Jesus, I see that You treat me in the same manner. I have despised and betrayed You, and You do not cast me off. You regard me with love, You admit me even to Your table of the Holy Communion. My dear Savior, oh that I had always loved You! And how shall I be ever again able to depart from Your feet and renounce Your love?

Meditation 27: Fourth Monday of Lent

The Sufferings of Jesus Were Extreme

Saint Ambrose, writing of the passion of Our Lord, says that Jesus Christ has followers, but no equals.[138] The saints have endeavored to imitate Jesus Christ in suffering, to render themselves like Him, but whoever attained to equaling Him in His sufferings? He truly suffered for us more than all the penitents, all the anchorites, all the martyrs have suffered because God laid upon Him the weight of a rigorous satisfaction to the divine justice for all the sins of men: *The Lord laid on Him the iniquity of us all.*[139] And, as Saint Peter writes, Jesus bore all our sins upon the cross, to pay our punishment with His most holy body: *He Himself bore our sins in His own body on the tree.*[140] Saint Thomas

---

[138]   *In Lucam*, chapter 23.
[139]   Is. 53:6.
[140]   1 Ptr. 2:24.

writes that Jesus Christ, in redeeming us, not only accomplished the virtue and infinite merit which belonged to His sufferings, but chose to suffer a depth of pain which might be sufficient to satisfy abundantly and rigorously for all the sins of the human race.[141] And Saint Bonaventure writes: "He chose to suffer as much pain as if He Himself had committed all our sins." God Himself thought right to aggravate the pains of Jesus Christ, until they were equal to the entire payment of all our debts, and thus the prophecy of Isaiah was fulfilled: *The Lord was pleased to bruise Him in infirmity.*[142]

When we read the lives of the martyrs, it seems at first as if some of them had suffered pains more bitter than those of Jesus Christ, but Saint Bonaventure says that the pains of no martyr could ever equal in acuteness the pains of our Savior, which were more acute than all other pains.[143] In like manner, Saint Thomas writes that the sufferings of Christ were the most severe pains that can be felt in this present life.[144] Upon which Saint Laurence Justinian writes that in each of the torments which Our Lord endured, on account of the agony and intensity of the suffering, He suffered as much as all the tortures of the martyrs.[145] And all this was predicted by King David in a few words, when, speaking in the person of Christ, he said, *Your wrath is strong*

---

[141]   See *S. T.*, III, q. 46, a. 6.
[142]   Is. 53:10.
[143]   *In Libros Sententiarum*, l. 3, d. 16, a. 1, q. 2.
[144]   See *S. T.*, III, q. 46, a. 6.
[145]   *De Tr. Chr. Ag. c.* 19.

over Me . . . Your terrors have troubled Me.[146] Thus all the wrath
of God, which He had conceived against our sins, poured itself
out upon the person of Jesus Christ, and thus we must interpret
what the Apostle said, *He was made a curse for us*[147]—that is, the
object of all the curses deserved by our sins.

---

[146] Ps. 87:8, 17.
[147] Gal. 3:13.

MEDITATION 28: FOURTH TUESDAY OF LENT

JESUS'S INTERIOR SUFFERINGS

Hitherto, also, we have spoken only of the outward bodily pains of Jesus Christ. And who can ever explain and comprehend the inward pains of His soul, which a thousand times exceeded His outward pains? This inward torment was such that in the Garden of Gethsemane it caused a sweat of blood to pour forth from all His body, and compelled Him to say that this was enough to slay Him: *My soul is sorrowful even unto death.*[148] And since this anguish was enough to cause death, why did He not die? Saint Thomas answers that He did not die because He Himself prevented His own death, being ready to preserve His life in order to give it in a while upon the tree of the cross. This sorrow also, which most deeply afflicted Jesus Christ in the garden, afflicted Him also throughout His whole life, since, from the first moment when He began to live, He had ever before His

---

[148] Matt. 26:38.

eyes the causes of His inward grief, among which the most afflicting was the sight of the ingratitude of men towards the love which He showed them in His passion.

Nevertheless, an angel came to comfort Him in the garden, as Saint Luke relates.[149] Yet Venerable Bede says that this comfort, instead of lightening His pains, increased them. The angel, indeed, strengthened Him to endure with greater constancy for the salvation of men; upon which Bede remarks that Jesus was then strengthened for suffering, by a representation of the greatness of the fruits of His passion, without the least diminution of the greatness of His sufferings. Therefore the Evangelist relates that immediately after the appearance of the angel, Jesus Christ was in an agony and sweated blood in such abundance that it fell to the ground.[150]

Saint Bonaventure further relates that the agony of Jesus then reached its height so that our afflicted Lord, at the sight of the anguish that He must suffer at the termination of His life now come, was so terrified that He prayed His divine Father that He might be delivered from it: *Father, if it be possible, let this cup pass from Me.*[151] Yet He said this, not that He might be delivered from the pains, for He had already offered Himself to suffer them—*He was offered, because He Himself willed*—but to teach us to understand the agony which He experienced in

---

149   See Luke 22:43.
150   See Luke 22:43–44.
151   Matt. 26:39.

enduring this death so bitter to the senses; while in His will, in order to accomplish the will of His Father, in order to obtain for us the salvation He so ardently desired, He immediately added: *Nevertheless, not as I will, but as You will.*[152] And He continued thus to pray and to resign Himself for the space of three hours: *He prayed the third time, saying the same words.*[153]

[152] Matt. 26:39.
[153] Matt. 26:44.

MEDITATION 29: FOURTH WEDNESDAY OF LENT

THE DESOLATE LIFE OF JESUS CHRIST

The life of our loving Redeemer was all full of desolation, and bereft of every comfort. The life of Jesus was that great ocean which was all bitter, without a single drop of sweetness or consolation: *For great as the sea is your destruction.*[154] This is what was revealed by Our Lord to Saint Margaret of Cortona when He said to her that in His whole life He never experienced sensible consolation.

The sadness which He felt in the garden of Gethsemane was so great that it was sufficient to take away His life. *My soul,* He said, *is sorrowful even unto death.*[155] This sadness afflicted Him not only in the garden but it always filled His soul with

---

[154] Lam. 2:13.
[155] Matt. 26:38.

desolation from the first moment of His conception: for, all the
pains and ignominies which He was to suffer until death were
always present to Him.

But the extreme affliction which He suffered during His
whole life arose not so much from the knowledge of all the sufferings He was to endure in His life, and especially at death, as
from the sight of all the sins which men would commit after His
death. He came to abolish sin and to save souls from hell by His
death, but after all His cruel sufferings, He saw all the sins which
men would commit, and the sight of each sin, being clearly before His mind while He lived here below, was to Him, as Saint
Bernadine of Sienna writes, a source of immense affliction.[156]
This was the sorrow which was always before His eyes, and kept
Him always in desolation: *My sorrow is continually before Me.*[157]
Saint Thomas teaches that the sight of the sins of men, and of
the multitude of souls that would bring themselves to perdition,
excited in Jesus Christ a sorrow which surpassed the sorrow of
all penitents, even of those who died of pure grief. The holy martyrs have suffered great torments; they have borne to be tortured
with iron hooks, and nails, and red-hot plates, but God always
sweetened their pains by interior consolations. But no martyrdom has been more painful than that of Jesus Christ; for His
pain and sadness were pure, unmitigated pain and sorrow, without the smallest comfort. "The greatness of Christ's suffering,"

---

[156]   T. 2 s. 56, a. 1, c. 1.
[157]   Ps. 37:18.

says the Angelic Doctor, "is estimated from the pureness of His pain and sadness."[158]

Such was the life of our Redeemer, and such His death, all full of desolation. Dying on the cross bereft of all comfort, He sought someone to console Him, but He found none. *I looked for one . . . that would comfort Me, and I found none.*[159] He found only scoffers and blasphemers, who said to Him: *If You be the Son of God, come down from the cross. . . . He saved others, Himself He cannot save.*[160] Hence, our afflicted Lord, finding Himself abandoned by all, turned to His Eternal Father: but seeing that His Father too had abandoned Him, He cried out with a loud voice, and sweetly complained of His Father's abandonment, saying, *My God, My God, why have You forsaken Me?*[161]

Thus our Savior terminated His life, dying, as David had foretold, immersed in a tempest of ignominies and sorrows: *I am come into the depth of the sea, and a tempest has overwhelmed Me.*[162]

When we are in desolation, let us console ourselves by the desolate death of Jesus Christ: let us offer Him our desolation in union with that which He, an innocent God, suffered on Calvary for the love of us.

---

[158] See *S. T.*, III, q. 46, a. 6.
[159] Ps. 68:21.
[160] Matt. 27:40–42.
[161] Matt. 27:46.
[162] Ps. 68:3.

Ah, my Jesus, who will not love You when He sees You die in such desolation, consumed by sorrows, in order to pay our debts? Behold me: I am one of the executioners, who have, by my sins, so grievously afflicted You during Your whole life. But, since You invite me to repentance, grant that I may feel at least a part of that sorrow which You felt during Your passion for my sins. How can I, who have by my sins so much afflicted You during Your life, seek after pleasures? No, I do not ask for pleasures and delights; I ask of You tears and sorrow: make me, during the remainder of my life, weep continually for the offenses that I have given You. I embrace Your feet, O my crucified and desolate Jesus: in embracing them, I wish to die. O afflicted Mary, pray to Jesus for me.

MEDITATION 30: FOURTH THURSDAY OF LENT

JESUS TREATED AS THE LAST OF MEN

We have seen Him, says the Prophet Isaiah, *despised and the most abject of men, a man of sorrows.*[163] This great prodigy was once seen on earth; the Son of God, the king of heaven, the Lord of the whole world, despised as the most abject of all men.

Saint Anselm[164] says that Jesus Christ wished to be humbled and despised in such a manner that it would be impossible for Him to endure greater humiliations or contempt. He was treated as a person of mean condition. *Is not this,* said the Jews, *the carpenter's son?*[165] He was despised on account of His country: *Can anything good come from Nazareth?*[166] He was held up as a

---

163 Is. 53:2–3.
164 *In Philippenses* 2.
165 Matt. 13:55.
166 John 1:46.

madman: *He is mad; why hear you Him?*[167] He was considered to
be a glutton and a friend of wine: *Behold a man that is a glutton
and a drinker of wine.*[168] He was called a sorcerer: *By the prince of
devils He casts out devils.*[169] And also a heretic: *Do we not say well
that You are a Samaritan?*[170]

But during His passion He suffered still greater insults. He
was treated as a blasphemer: when He declared that He was the
Son of God, Caiaphas said to the other priests, *Behold, now you
have heard the blasphemy: what think you? But they answering said,
He is guilty of death.*[171] As soon as He was declared guilty of blasphemy, some began to spit in His face, and others to buffet Him.[172]
Then, indeed, was fulfilled the prediction of Isaiah: *I have given
My body to the strikers, and My cheeks to them that plucked them; I
have not turned away My face from them that rebuked Me and spit
upon Me.*[173] He was next treated as a false prophet: *Prophesy unto
us, O Christ; who is he that struck You?*[174] The injury done Him by
His disciple Peter, who denied Him three times, and swore that
he had never known Him, added to the pain which our Savior
suffered from the ignominies of that night.

---

[167]   John 10:20.
[168]   Luke 7:34.
[169]   Matt. 9:34.
[170]   John 8:48.
[171]   Matt. 26:65–66.
[172]   See Matt. 26:67.
[173]   Is. 50:6.
[174]   Matt. 26:68.

Let us, O devout souls, go to our afflicted Lord in that prison in which He is abandoned by all, and accompanied only by His enemies, who contend with each other in insulting and maltreating Him. Let us thank Him for all that He suffers for us with so much patience, and let us console Him by acts of sorrow for the insults that we have offered to Him; for, we too have treated Him with contempt, and by our sins we have denied Him, and declared that we knew Him not.

Ah, my amiable Redeemer, I would wish to die of grief at the thought of having given so much pain to Your heart, which has loved me so ardently. Ah, forget the great offenses I have offered You, and look at me with that loving look which You cast on Peter after he denied You, and which made him bewail his sins unceasingly till death. O great Son of God, O infinite love, who suffers for the very men that hate and maltreat You, You are adored by the angels. You are infinite majesty; You would confer a great honor on men by permitting them to kiss Your feet. But, O God, how have You borne on that night to be made an object of mockery to so vile a rabble? My despised Jesus, make me suffer contempt for Your sake. How can I refuse insults, when I see that You, my God, have borne so many for the love of me? Ah, my crucified Jesus, make me know You and love You.

MEDITATION 31: FOURTH FRIDAY OF LENT

THE PASSION OF JESUS CHRIST IS OUR CONSOLATION

Who can ever give us so much consolation in this valley of tears as Jesus crucified? What can sweeten the punctures of remorse, arising from the remembrance of our past sins, better than the consideration that Jesus Christ has voluntarily suffered death in order to atone for our sins? *He*, says the Apostle, *gave Himself for our sins.*[175]

In all the persecutions, calumnies, insults, spoliations of property and honors which happen to us in this life, who is better able to give us strength to bear them with patience and resignation than Jesus Christ, who was despised, calumniated, and poor, who died on a cross, naked, and abandoned by all?

---

[175] Gal. 1:4.

What more consoling in infirmities than the sight of Jesus crucified? In our sickness we find ourselves on a comfortable bed, but when Jesus was sick on the cross on which He died, He had no other bed than a hard tree, to which He was fastened by three nails, no other pillow on which to rest His head than the crown of thorns, which continued to torment Him till He expired.

In our sickness, we have around our bed friends and relatives to sympathize with us and to divert us. Jesus died in the midst of enemies, who insulted and mocked Him as a malefactor and seducer, even when He was in the very agony of death. Certainly, there is nothing so well calculated as the life of Jesus crucified to console a sick man in his sufferings, particularly if he finds himself abandoned by others. Ah, to unite, in his infirmity, his own pains to the pains of Jesus Christ is the greatest comfort that a poor sick man can enjoy.

In the anguish caused at death by the assaults of hell, the sight of past sins, and the account to be rendered in a short time at the divine tribunal, the only consolation which a dying Christian, combating with death, can have consists in embracing the crucifix, saying, my Jesus and my Redeemer, You are my love and my hope.

In a word, all the graces, lights, inspirations, holy desires, devout affections, sorrow for sins, good resolutions, divine love, and hope of paradise that God bestows upon us are fruits and gifts which come to us through the passion of Jesus Christ.

Ah, my Jesus, if You, my Savior, had not died for me, what hope could I, who have so often turned my back upon You and so often deserved hell, entertain of going to behold Your beautiful countenance in the land of bliss, among so many innocent virgins, among so many holy martyrs, among the apostles and seraphs? It is Your passion, then, that makes me hope, in spite of my sins, that I too will one day reach the society of the saints and of Your holy Mother, to sing Your mercies, and to thank and love You forever in paradise. Such, O Jesus, is my hope. *The mercies of the Lord I will sing forever.*[176] Mary, Mother of God, pray to Jesus for me.

---

[176] Ps. 88:2.

JESUS MAKES HIS TRIUMPHANT ENTRY INTO JERUSALEM

The time of His passion being now at hand, our Redeemer departs from Bethany to go to Jerusalem. On drawing nigh to that ungrateful city, He beheld it, and wept: *Beholding the city, He wept over it.*[177] He wept because He foresaw its ruin, which would be the consequence of the stupendous crime of taking away the life of the Son of God, of which that people would shortly become guilty. Ah, my Jesus, when You were then weeping over that city You were weeping also over my soul, beholding the ruin which I have brought upon myself by my sins, constraining You to condemn me to hell, even after Your having died to save me. Oh, leave it to me to weep over the great evil

---

[177] Luke 19:41.

of which I have been guilty in despising You, the greatest of all goods. Have mercy upon me.

Jesus Christ enters the city: the people go forth to meet Him; they receive Him with acclamations and rejoicings, and in order to do Him honor, some of them strew branches of palms along the road, while others spread out their garments for Him to pass over. Oh, who would ever then have said that that Lord, now recognized as the Messiah, and welcomed with so many demonstrations of respect, the next time that He appeared along the self-same ways would be under sentence of death, and with a cross upon His shoulders? Ah, my beloved Jesus, these people now receive You with acclamations, saying, *Hosanna to the Son of David! Blessed is He that comes in the name of the Lord!*[178] Glory to the Son of David! Blessed be He who comes in the name of God for our salvation! And then they will raise their voices insultingly to Pilate to take You out of the world, and cause You to die upon a cross: *Away with Him! Away with Him! Crucify Him!*[179] Go, my soul, and lovingly say to Him, *Blessed is He that comes in the name of the Lord!* Blessed forever be You that are come, O Savior of the world, for, otherwise, we had all been lost. O my Savior, save me!

When the evening, however, was come, after all those acclamations, there was no one found who would invite Him to

---

[178] Matt. 21:9.
[179] John 19:15.

lodge in his house so that He was obliged to retrace His steps to Bethany.

O my beloved Redeemer, if others will not give You a welcome, I desire to welcome You into my poor heart. At one time, I, unhappily, expelled You from my soul, but I now prize to have You with me more than the possession of all the treasures of earth. I love You, O my Savior; what power shall ever be able to separate me from my love of You? Sin only, but from this sin it is Yours to deliver me, by Your help, O my Jesus, and thine too, by your intercession, O Mary, my Mother.

MEDITATION 33: PASSION SUNDAY

JESUS PRAYS IN THE GARDEN

Jesus, knowing that the hour of His passion had now come, after having washed the feet of His disciples and instituted the most Holy Sacrament of the Altar—wherein He left us His whole self—goes to the Garden of Gethsemane, whither He already knew that His enemies would come to take Him. He there betakes Himself to prayer, and lo! He finds Himself assailed by a great dread, by a great repugnance, and by a great sadness: *He began to be afraid, to be weary, and sorrowful.*[180] There came upon Him, first, a great dread of the bitter death which He would have to suffer on Calvary, and of all the anguish and desolations by which it would be accompanied. During the actual course of His passion, the scourges, the thorns, the nails, and the rest of His tortures came upon Him but one at a time; whereas, in the garden, they all came upon Him together at once, crowding into

---

[180]   Mark 14:33; Matt. 26:37.

His memory in order to torment Him. For His love of us He embraced them all, but in embracing them, He trembles and is in agony: *Being in an agony, He prayed the longer.*[181]

There comes upon Him, moreover, a great repugnance to that which He has to suffer so that He prays His Father to deliver Him from it: *My Father, if it be possible, let this chalice pass away from Me.*[182] He prayed thus to teach us that in our tribulations we may indeed beg of God to deliver us from them, but we ought at the same time to refer ourselves to His will and to say, as Jesus then said, *Not, however, as I will, but as You will.*[183] Yes, my Jesus, Your will, not mine, be done. I embrace all the crosses that You will send me. You, innocent as You are, have suffered so much for love of me; it is but just that I, who am a sinner, and deserving of hell, should suffer for love of You that which You ordain.

There came upon Him, likewise, a sadness so great that it would have been enough to cause Him to die, had He not, of Himself, kept death away, in order to die for us after having suffered more: *My soul is sorrowful even unto death.*[184] This great sadness was occasioned by the sight of the future ungratefulness of men, who, instead of corresponding to so great a love on His part, would offend Him by so many sins, the sight of which

---

[181] Luke 22:43.
[182] Matt. 26:39.
[183] Matt. 26:39.
[184] Mark 14:34.

caused Him to sweat in streams of blood: *And His sweat became as drops of blood trickling down upon the ground.*[185]

So, then, O my Jesus, it is not the executioners, the scourges, the thorns, or the cross that have been so cruel, the cruelty lies in my sins, which afflicted You so much in the garden. Give me, then, a share of that sorrow and abhorrence which You experienced in the garden that so, even to my death, I may bitterly weep for the offenses that I have given You. I love You, O my Jesus; receive with kindness a sinner who wishes to love You. Recommend me, O Mary, to this your Son, who is in affliction and sadness for love of me.

---

[185] Luke 22:44.

MEDITATION **34**: PASSION MONDAY

JESUS IS APPREHENDED AND LED BEFORE CAIAPHAS

The Lord, knowing that the Jews who were coming to take Him were now at hand, rose up from prayer and went to meet them, and so, without reluctance, He let them take Him and bind Him: *They apprehended Jesus, and bound Him.*[186] O amazement! A God bound as a criminal by His own creatures! Behold, my soul, how some of them seize hold of His hands; others put the handcuffs on Him; and others smite Him; and the innocent Lamb lets Himself be bound and struck at their will, and says not a word: *He was offered because it was His own will, and opened not His mouth. He is led as a sheep to the slaughter.*[187] He neither speaks nor utters complaint, since He had already offered Himself up to die for us; and, therefore, did that

---

[186] John 18:12.
[187] Is. 53:7.

Lamb let Himself be bound and led to death without opening
His mouth.

Jesus enters Jerusalem bound. Those who were asleep in
their beds, at the noise of the crowd passing by, awake and in-
quire who that might be whom they are taking along in custody,
and they are told in reply, "It is Jesus of Nazareth, who has been
found out to be an impostor and seducer." They bring Him up
before Caiaphas, who is pleased at seeing Him, and asks Him
about His disciples and about His doctrine. Jesus replies that
He has spoken openly so that He calls upon the Jews themselves, who were standing around Him, to bear their testimony
as to what He has said: *Behold, these know what I have said.*[188]
But upon this reply, one of the officials of the court gives Him a
blow in the face, saying, *Do You answer the high priest so?*[189] But,
O God, how does a reply, so humble and gentle, deserve so great
an insult?

Ah, my Jesus, You suffer it all in order to pay the penalty
of the insults that I have offered to Your heavenly Father. The
high priest, in the next place, conjures Him, in the name of God,
to say whether He be truly the Son of God. Jesus answered in
the affirmative, that such He was, and Caiaphas, on hearing this,
instead of prostrating himself upon the floor to adore his God,
rends his garments and, turning to the other priests, says, *What
more need have we of witnesses? Behold, you have now heard His*

---

[188]   John 18:21.
[189]   John 18:22.

blasphemy: what is your opinion? And they unanimously replied, *He is guilty of death.*[190] And then, as the Evangelists relate, they all began to spit in His face, and to abuse Him, and slapping Him with their hands, and striking Him with their fists, and then, tying a piece of cloth over His face, they turned Him into ridicule, saying, *Prophesy to us, You Christ; who is it that smote You?* Thus writes Saint Matthew. And Saint Mark writes, *And some began to spit upon Him, and to cover His face, and to deal upon Him blows, and to say to Him, Prophesy. And the officers did smite Him with the palms of their hands.*[191]

Behold Yourself, O my Jesus, become, upon this night, the butt of the rabble. And how can men see You in such humiliation for love of them, and not love You? And how have I been able to go so far as to outrage You by so many sins, after that You have suffered so much for me? Forgive me, O my love, for I will not displease You more. I love You, my supreme Good, and I repent above every other evil of having despised You. O Mary, my Mother, pray your ill-treated Son to pardon me.

---

[190]   Matt. 26:65–66.
[191]   Matt. 26:68; Mark 14:65.

MEDITATION 35: PASSION TUESDAY

JESUS IS LED BEFORE PILATE AND HEROD

The morning being come, they lead Jesus to Pilate, that he may pronounce upon Him the sentence of death. But Pilate is aware that Jesus is innocent, and, therefore, he tells the Jews that he can find no reason why he should condemn Him. However, on seeing them obstinate in their desire for His death, he referred Him to the court of Herod. Herod, on seeing Jesus before Him, desired to see some one of the Lord's great miracles, of which he had heard accounts, wrought in his presence. The Lord would not vouchsafe so much as an answer to the questions of that audacious man. Alas for that poor soul to which God speaks no more!

O my Redeemer, such, too, were my deserts for not having obeyed so many calls of Yours; I deserved that You should not speak to me more, and that You should leave me to myself: but no, my Jesus, You have not abandoned me yet. Speak to me, then: *Speak, Lord, for Your servant hears;*[192] tell me what You desire of me, for I will do all to please You.

Herod, seeing that Jesus gave him no answer, drove Him away from his house with scorn, turning Him into ridicule with all the persons of his court, and in order to load Him with the greater contempt, he had Him clothed in a white garment, so treating Him like a fool, and thus he sent Him back again to Pilate: *He despised and mocked Him, putting on Him a white garment, and sent Him again to Pilate.*[193] Behold how Jesus, clad in that robe which makes Him a laughing-stock, is borne on along the streets of Jerusalem. O my despised Savior, this additional wrong, of being treated as a fool, was still wanting to You! If, then, the divine wisdom is so treated by the world, happy is he who cares nothing for the world's approbation, and desires nothing but to know Jesus crucified, and to love sufferings and contempt, saying, with the Apostle: *For I judged not myself to know anything among you, but Jesus Christ, and Him crucified.*[194]

The Jews had the right of demanding from the Roman governor the liberation of a criminal on the feast of the Passover. Pilate, therefore, asked the people which of the two they would wish to have liberated, Jesus or Barabbas: *Whom will you that I release to you, Barabbas or Jesus?*[195] Barabbas was a wicked

---

[192]   1 Kgs. 3:9 [1 Sm. 3:9].
[193]   Luke 23:11.
[194]   1 Cor. 2:2.
[195]   Matt. 27:17.

wretch, a murderer, a thief, and held in abhorrence by all: Jesus was innocent, but the Jews cry aloud for Barabbas to live and for Jesus to die.

Ah, my Jesus, so too have I said, whenever I have deliberately offended You for some satisfaction of my own, preferring before You that miserable pleasure of mine, and in order not to lose it, contenting myself to lose You, O infinite Good. But now I love You above every other good, and more than my life itself. Have compassion upon me, O God of mercy. And do you, O Mary, be my advocate.

JESUS IS SCOURGED AT THE PILLAR

Then Pilate, therefore, took Jesus and scourged Him.[196] O you unjust judge, you have declared Him innocent, and then you condemn Him to so cruel and so ignominious a punishment! Behold, now, my soul, how, after this unjust decree, the executioners seize hold of the divine Lamb; they take Him to the praetorium and bind Him with ropes to the pillar.

O you blessed ropes that bound the hands of my sweet Redeemer to that pillar, bind likewise this wretched heart of mine to His divine heart, that so I may, from this day forth, neither seek for nor desire anything but what He wishes.

Behold how they now lay hold of the scourges and, at a given sign, begin to strike, in every part, that sacred flesh, which at first assumes a livid appearance and then is covered all over with

---

[196] John 19:1.

blood that flows from every pore. Alas, the scourges and the executioners' hands are all now dyed in blood, and with blood is the
ground all drenched. But, O God, through the violence of the
blows, not only does the blood, but pieces of the very flesh of Jesus Christ go flying through the air. That divine body is already
but one mass of wounds, and yet do those barbarians continue
to add blow to blow and pain to pain. And all this while, what
is Jesus doing? He speaks not; He complains not, but patiently
endures that great torture in order to appease the divine justice
that was wroth against us: *As a lamb before the shearer is dumb, so
opened He not His mouth.*[197] Go quickly, O my soul, go and wash
yourself in that divine blood.

My beloved Savior, I behold You all torn in pieces for me;
no longer, therefore, can I doubt that You love me, and love me
greatly, too. Every wound of Yours is a sure token on Your part of
Your love, which with too much reason demands my love. You,
O my Jesus, without reserve, give me Your blood; it is but just
that I, without reserve, should give You all my heart. Do You,
then, accept of it, and make it to be ever faithful.

O my God, had Jesus Christ not suffered more than a single
blow for love of me, I ought yet to have been burning with love
for Him, saying, A God has been willing to be struck for me! But
no: He contented not Himself with a single blow; but, to pay the
penalty due to my sins, He was willing to have His whole body
torn to shreds, as Isaiah had already foretold: *He was bruised*

---

[197]   Acts 8:32.

for our iniquities;[198] and that even until He looked like a leper covered with wounds from head to foot: *And we thought Him to be, as it were, a leper.*[199] While, then, O my soul, Jesus was being scourged, He was thinking of you, and offering to God those bitter sufferings of His in order to deliver you from the eternal scourges of hell. O God of love, how have I been able to live so many years, in time past, without loving You? O you wounds of Jesus, wound me with love towards a God who has loved me so much! O Mary, O Mother of graces, gain for me this love!

---

[198] Is. 53:5.
[199] Is. 53:4.

MEDITATION 37: PASSION THURSDAY

JESUS IS CROWNED
WITH THORNS

When the soldiers had finished the scourging of Jesus Christ, they all assembled together in the praetorium, and stripping His own clothes off Him again in order to turn Him into ridicule and to make Him into a mock king, they put upon Him an old ragged mantle of a reddish color to represent the royal purple, in His hand a reed to represent a scepter, and upon His head a bundle of thorns to represent a crown, but fashioned like a helmet so as to fit close upon the whole of His sacred head. *Stripping Him, they put a scarlet cloak about Him, and plaiting a crown of thorns they put it upon His head, and a reed in His right hand.*[200] And when the thorns, by the pressure of their hands alone, could not be made to penetrate deeper into that divine head which they were piercing, with the self-same

---

200 Matt. 27:28–29.

reed, and with all their might, they battered down that barbarous crown: *And spitting upon Him, they took the reed, and struck
His head.*[201] O ungrateful thorns, do you thus torture your Creator? But what thorns? What thorns? You wicked thoughts of
mine; it is you that have pierced the head of my Redeemer.

I detest, O my Jesus, and I abhor, more than I do death itself, the evil consent by which I have so often grieved You, my
God, who are so good. But since You make me know how much
You have loved me, You alone will I love, You alone. O my God,
how the blood is now streaming down from that pierced head
over the face and the breast of Jesus! And You, my Savior, do
not even utter a complaint of such unjust cruelties! You are the
King of heaven and of earth, but now, my Jesus, You are brought
down so low as to appear before us a king of derision and of
sorrows, being made the laughing-stock of all Jerusalem. But the
prophecy of Jeremiah had to be fulfilled, that You would one day
have Your fill of sorrows and shame: *He will give His cheek to the
smiter, He will be satiated with reproaches.*[202] O Jesus, my love, in
time past I have despised You, but now I prize You, and I love
You with all my heart, and I desire to die for love of You.

But no; these men for whom You are suffering have not yet
their fill of torturing and making game of You. After having thus
tortured You, and dressed You up as a mock king, they bend
their knee before You and scornfully address You: *Hail to You, O*

---

[201]   Matt. 27:30.
[202]   Lam. 3:30.

King of the Jews. And then, with shouts of laughter, they deal out more blows upon You, thus rendering twofold the anguish of the head already pierced by the thorns: *And bowing the knee before Him, they derided Him, saying, Hail, King of the Jews; and they gave Him blows.*[203] At least go, O my soul, and recognize Jesus for what He is, the King of kings and Lord of lords, and return thanks to Him, and love Him, now that you behold Him become, for love of you, the king of sorrows. O my Lord, keep not in Your remembrance the griefs which I have caused You. I now love You more than myself. You only deserve all my love, and, therefore, You only do I wish to love. I fear, on account of my weaknesses, but it is for You to give me the strength to execute my desire. And you, too, O Mary, must help me by your prayers.

---

[203]   Matt. 27:29; John 19:3.

PILATE EXHIBITS JESUS TO THE PEOPLE

Jesus having again been brought and set before Pilate, he beheld Him so wounded and disfigured by the scourges and the thorns that he thought, by showing Him to them, to move the people to compassion. He therefore went out into the portico, bringing with Him the afflicted Lord, and said, *Behold the Man.*[204] As though he would say, "Go now, and rest content with that which this poor innocent one has already suffered. Behold Him brought to so low a state that He cannot long survive. Go your way, and leave Him, for He can but have a short time to live." Do you too, my soul, behold your Lord in that portico, bound and half naked, covered only with wounds and blood, and consider to what your Shepherd has reduced Himself in order to save you, a sheep that was lost.

---

[204] John 19:5.

At the same time that Pilate is exhibiting the wounded Jesus to the Jews, the Eternal Father is from heaven inviting us to turn our eyes to behold Jesus Christ in such a condition, and in like manner says to us, *Behold the Man!* O men, this man whom you behold thus wounded and set at naught, He is My beloved Son, who is suffering all this in order to pay the penalty of your sins; behold Him, and love Him. O my God and my Father, I do behold Your Son, and I thank Him, and love Him, and hope to love Him always, but do You, I pray You, behold Him also, and for love of this Your Son have mercy upon me, pardon me, and give me the grace never to love anything apart from You.

But what is it that the Jews reply, on their beholding that king of sorrows? They raise a shout and say, *Crucify Him, crucify Him!*[205] And seeing that Pilate, notwithstanding their clamor, was seeking a means to release Him, they worked upon his fears by telling him: *If you release this Man, you are not Caesar's friend.*[206] Pilate still makes resistance, and replies, *Shall I crucify your King?* And their answer was, *We have no king but Caesar.*[207]

Ah, my adorable Jesus, these men will not recognize You for their King, and tell You that they wish for no other king but Caesar. I acknowledge You to be my King and God, and I protest that I wish for no other king of my heart but You, my love, and my one and only good. Wretch that I am! I at one time refused

---

[205] John 19:6.
[206] John 19:12.
[207] John 19:15.

You for my King and declared that I did not wish to serve You, but now I wish You alone to have dominion over my will. Make it obey You in all that You ordain. O will of God, you are my love. O Mary, pray for me. Your prayers are not rejected.

MEDITATION 39: PASSION SATURDAY

JESUS IS CONDEMNED BY PILATE

Behold, at last, how Pilate, after having so often declared the innocence of Jesus, declares it now anew, and protesting that he is innocent of the blood of that just man—*I am innocent of the blood of this just man*[208]—after all this he pronounces the sentence and condemns Him to death. Oh, what injustice—such as the world has never seen! At the very time that the judge declares the accused one to be innocent, he condemns Him. Ah, my Jesus, You do not deserve death, but it is I that deserve it. Since, then, it is Your will to make satisfaction for me, it is not Pilate but Your Father Himself who justly condemns You to pay the penalty that was my due. I love You, O Eternal Father, who condemns Your innocent Son in order to liberate me, who am

---

[208] Matt. 27:24.

the guilty one. I love You, O Eternal Son, who accepts the death which I, a sinner, have deserved.

Pilate, after having pronounced sentence upon Jesus, delivers Him over to the hands of the Jews to the end that they may do with Him whatsoever they please: *He delivered Jesus up to their will.*[209] Such truly is the course of things. When an innocent one is condemned, there are no limits to the punishment, but He is left in the hands of His enemies, that they may make Him suffer and die according to their own pleasure. You now endure, you miserable men, and will endure, even to the end of the world, the penalty of that innocent blood.

O my Jesus, have mercy upon me, who by my sins have also been a cause of Your death. But I do not wish to be obstinate; I wish to bewail the evil treatment that I have given You, and I wish to love You—always, always, always!

Behold, the unjust sentence of death upon a cross is read over in the presence of the condemned Lord. He listens to it, and all-submissive to the will of the Father, He obediently and humbly accepts it: *He humbled Himself, becoming obedient unto death, and that the death of the cross.*[210] Pilate says on earth, "Let Jesus die," and the Eternal Father, in like manner, says from heaven, "Let My Son die," and the Son Himself makes answer, "Behold Me! I obey; I accept death, and death upon a cross."

---

[209]   Luke 23:25.
[210]   Phil. 2:8.

O my beloved Redeemer! You accept the death that was my due. Blessed for evermore be Your mercy: I return You my most hearty thanks for it. But since You who are innocent accept the death of the cross for me, I, who am a sinner, accept that death which You destine to be mine, together with all the pains that shall accompany it, and from this time forth I unite it to Your death and offer it up to Your Eternal Father. You have died for love of me, and I wish to die for love of You. Ah, by the merits of Your holy death, make me die in Your grace, and burning with holy love for You. Mary, my hope, be mindful of me.

MEDITATION 40: PALM SUNDAY

JESUS CARRIES THE CROSS TO CALVARY

The sentence upon our Savior having been published, they straightway seize hold of Him in their fury: they strip Him anew of that purple rag, and put His own raiment upon Him, to lead Him away to be crucified on Calvary—the place appropriated for the execution of criminals: *They took off the cloak from Him, and put on Him His own garments, and led Him away to crucify Him.*[211] They then lay hold of two rough beams and quickly make them into a cross and order Him to carry it on His shoulders to the place of His punishment. What cruelty to lay upon the criminal the gibbet on which he has to die! But this is Your lot, O my Jesus, because You have taken my sins upon Yourself.

Jesus refuses not the cross; with love, He embraces it, as being the altar whereon is destined to be completed the sacrifice

---

[211] Matt. 27:31.

of His life for the salvation of men: *And bearing His own cross, He went forth to that place which is called Calvary.*[212] The condemned criminals now come forth from Pilate's residence, and in the midst of them there goes also our condemned Lord. O that sight, which filled both heaven and earth with amazement! To see the Son of God going to die for the sake of those very men from whose hands He is receiving His death! Behold the prophecy fulfilled: *And I was as a meek lamb, that is carried to be a victim.*[213] The appearance that Jesus made on this journey was so pitiable that the Jewish women, on beholding Him, followed Him in tears: *They bewailed and lamented Him.*[214]

O my Redeemer, by the merits of this sorrowful journey of Yours, give me strength to bear my cross with patience. I accept all the sufferings and contempts which You destine for me to undergo. You have rendered them lovely and sweet by embracing them for love of us: give me strength to endure them with calmness.

Behold, my soul, now that your condemned Savior is passing, behold how He moves along, dripping with blood that keeps flowing from His still fresh wounds, crowned with thorns, and laden with the cross. Alas, how at every motion is the pain of all His wounds renewed! The cross, from the first moment, begins its torture, pressing heavily upon His wounded shoulders and

---

[212]   John 19:17.
[213]   Jer. 11:19.
[214]   Luke 23:27.

cruelly acting like a hammer upon the thorns of the crown. O God, at every step, how great are the sufferings! Let us meditate upon the sentiments of love wherewith Jesus, in this journey, is drawing nigh to Calvary, where death stands awaiting Him.

Ah, my Jesus, You are going to die for us. In time past I have turned my back upon You, and would that I could die of grief on this account! But for the future I have not the heart any more to leave You, O my Redeemer, my God, my love, my all! O Mary, my Mother, obtain for me strength to bear my cross in peace.

JESUS IS PLACED
UPON THE CROSS

No sooner had the Redeemer arrived, all suffering and wearied out, at Calvary, than they strip Him of His clothes—that now stick to His wounded flesh—and then cast Him down upon the cross. Jesus stretches forth His holy hands and at the same time offers up the sacrifice of His life to the eternal Father and prays of Him to accept it for the salvation of mankind. In the next place, the executioners savagely lay hold of the nails and hammers, and nailing His hands and His feet, they fasten Him to the cross. O you sacred hands, which by a mere touch have so often healed the sick, wherefore are they now nailing you upon this cross? O holy feet, which have encountered so much fatigue in your search after us lost sheep, wherefore do they now transfix you with so much pain? When a nerve is wounded in the human body, so great is the suffering that it occasions convulsions and fits of fainting: what, then, must not the suffering of Jesus have been in having nails driven through His hands and feet, parts which are most full of nerves and muscles!

O my sweet Savior, so much did the desire of seeing me saved and of gaining my love cost You! And I have so often ungratefully despised Your love for nothing, but now I prize it above every good.

The cross is now raised up, together with the Crucified, and they let it fall with a shock into the hole that had been made for it in the rock. It is then made firm by means of stones and pieces of wood, and Jesus remains hanging upon it, to leave His life thereon. The afflicted Savior, now about to die upon that bed of pain, and finding Himself in such desolation and misery, seeks for someone to console Him, but finds none. Surely, my Lord, those men will at least compassionate You now that You are dying! But no; I hear some outraging You, some ridiculing You, and others blaspheming You, saying to You, *"Come down from the cross if You are the Son of God... He has saved others, and now He cannot save Himself."*[215] Alas, you barbarians, He is now about to die, according as you desire; at least torment Him not with your revilings.

See how much your dying Redeemer is suffering upon that gibbet! Each member suffers its own pain, and the one cannot come to the help of the other. Alas, how does He experience in every moment the pains of death! Well may it be said that in

---

[215]   Matt. 27:40, 42.

those three hours during which Jesus was suffering His agony upon the cross, He suffered as many deaths as were the moments that He remained there. He finds not there even the slightest relief or repose, whether He lean His weight upon His hands or upon His feet; wheresoever He leans the pain is increased, His most holy body hanging suspended, as it does, from His very wounds themselves. Go, my soul, and tenderly draw nigh to that cross and kiss that altar whereon your Lord is dying a victim of love for you. Place yourself beneath His feet, and let that divine blood trickle down upon you.

Yes, my dear Jesus, let this blood wash me from all my sins, and set me all on fire with love towards You, my God, who have been willing to die for love of me. O suffering Mother, who stands at the foot of the cross, pray to Jesus for me.

MEDITATION 42: HOLY TUESDAY

JESUS UPON THE CROSS

Jesus on the cross! Behold the proof of the love of God; behold the final manifestation of Himself, which the Word Incarnate makes upon this earth—a manifestation of suffering indeed, but still more, a manifestation of love. Saint Francis of Paola, as he was one day meditating upon the divine Love in the person of Jesus Crucified, rapt in ecstasy, exclaimed aloud three times in these words, "O God—Love! O God—Love! O God—Love!" wishing hereby to signify that we shall never be able to comprehend how great has been the divine love towards us in willing to die for love of us.

O my beloved Jesus, if I behold Your body upon this cross, nothing do I see but wounds and blood, and then, if I turn my attention to Your heart, I find it to be all afflicted and in sorrow. Upon this cross I see it written that You are a king, but what tokens of majesty do You retain? I see not any royal throne save that of this tree of infamy; no other purple do I behold save Your wounded and bloody flesh; no other crown save this band of thorns that tortures You. Ah, how it all declares You to be the king of love! Yes, for this cross, these nails, this crown, and these wounds are, all of them, tokens of love.

Jesus, from the cross, asks us not so much for our compassion as for our love, and if even He asks our compassion, He asks it solely in order that the compassion may move us to love Him. As being infinite goodness, He already merits all our love, but when placed upon the cross, it seems as if He sought for us to love Him, at least out of compassion.

Ah, my Jesus, and who is there that will not love You while confessing You to be the God that You are and contemplating You upon the cross? Oh, what arrows of fire do You not dart at souls from that throne of love! Oh, how many hearts have You not drawn to Yourself from that cross of Yours! O wounds of my Jesus! O beautiful furnaces of love, admit me, too, among yourselves to burn, not indeed with that fire of hell which I have deserved but with holy flames of love for that God who has been willing to die for me, consumed by torments. O my dear Redeemer, receive back a sinner, who, sorrowing for having offended You, is now earnestly longing to love You. I love You, I love You, O infinite goodness, O infinite love. O Mary, O Mother of beautiful love, obtain for me a greater measure of love to consume me for that God who has died consumed of love for me.

THE WORDS SPOKEN BY JESUS UPON THE CROSS

While Jesus upon the cross is being outraged by that barbarous populace, what is it that He is doing? He is praying for them and saying, *O My Father, forgive them; for they know not what they do.*[216] O Eternal Father, hearken to this Your beloved Son, who, in dying, prays You to forgive me too, who have outraged You so much. Then Jesus, turning to the good thief, who prays Him to have mercy upon him, replies, *Today you shall be with Me in paradise.*[217] Oh, how true is that which the Lord spoke by the mouth of Ezekiel, that when a sinner repents of his faults, He, as it were, blots out from His memory all the offenses

---

[216] Luke 23:34.
[217] Luke 23:43.

of which he has been guilty: *But if the wicked do penance . . . I will not remember all his iniquities.*[218]

Oh, would that it were true, my Jesus, that I had never offended You! But since the evil is done, remember no more, I pray You, the displeasures that I have given You, and by that bitter death which You have suffered for me, take me to Your kingdom after my death, and while I live, let Your love ever reign within my soul.

Jesus, in His agony upon the cross, with every part of His body full of torture, and deluged with affliction in His soul, seeks for someone to console Him. He looks towards Mary, but that sorrowing Mother only adds by her grief to His affliction. He casts His eyes around Him and there is no one that gives Him comfort. He asks His Father for consolation, but the Father, beholding Him covered with all the sins of men, even He too abandons Him, and then it is that Jesus cries out with a loud voice: *Jesus cried out with a loud voice, saying, My God, My God, why have You forsaken Me?*[219] My God, My God, and why have You also abandoned Me? This abandonment by the eternal Father caused the death of Jesus Christ to be more bitter than any that has ever fallen to the lot of either penitent or martyr; for it was a death of perfect desolation and bereft of every kind of relief.

O my Jesus, how is it that I have been able to live so long a time in forgetfulness of You? I return You thanks that You have not been unmindful of me. Oh, I pray You ever to keep me in

---

[218] Ezech. 18:21–22.
[219] Matt. 27:46.

mind of the bitter death which You have embraced for love of me so that I may never be unmindful of the love which You have borne me!

Jesus then, knowing that His sacrifice was now completed, said that He was thirsty: *He said, I thirst.*[220] And the executioners then reached up to His mouth a sponge, filled with vinegar and gall. But, Lord, how is it that You make no complaint of those many pains which are taking away Your life, but complain only of Your thirst? Ah, I understand You, my Jesus; Your thirst is a thirst of love; because You love us, You desire to be beloved by us. Oh, help me to drive away from my heart all affections which are not for You; make me to love none other but You and to have no other desire save that of doing Your will. O will of God! You are my love. O Mary, my Mother, obtain for me the grace to wish for nothing but that which God wills.

---

[220] John 19:28.

MEDITATION 44: HOLY THURSDAY

JESUS DIES UPON THE CROSS

Behold how the loving Savior is now drawing nigh unto death. Behold, O my soul, those beautiful eyes growing dim, that face become all pallid, that heart all but ceasing to beat, and that sacred body now disposing itself to the final surrender of its life. After Jesus had received the vinegar, He said, *It is consummated.*[221] He then passed over in review before His eyes all the sufferings that He had undergone during His life, in the shape of poverty, contempt, and pain, and then offering them all up to the Eternal Father, He turned to Him and said, *It is finished.* My Father, behold by the sacrifice of My death, the work of the world's redemption, which You have laid upon Me, is now completed. And it seems as though, turning Himself again to us, He repeated, *It is finished*, as if He would have said, "O men, O men,

---

[221] John 19:30.

love Me, for I have done all; there is nothing more that I can do in order to gain your love."

Behold now, lastly, Jesus dies. Come, you angels of heaven, come and assist at the death of your King. And you, O sorrowing Mother Mary, draw nearer to the cross and fix your eyes yet more attentively on your Son, for He is now on the point of death. Behold how, after having commended His spirit to His eternal Father, He calls upon death, giving it permission to come to take away His life. *"Come, O death,"* says He to it, *"be quick and perform thine office; slay Me and save My flock."* The earth now trembles, the graves open, the veil of the temple is rent in twain. The strength of the dying Savior is failing through the violence of the sufferings; the warmth of His body is gradually diminishing; He gives up His body to death: He bows His head down upon His breast, He opens His mouth and dies: *And bowing His head, He gave up the ghost.*[222] The people behold Him expire, and observing that He no longer moves, they say, He is dead, He is dead, and to them the voice of Mary makes echo, while she too says, "Ah, my Son, You are, then, dead."

He is dead! O God, who is it that is dead? The author of life, the only-begotten Son of God, the Lord of the world—He is dead. O death, you were the amazement of heaven and of all nature. O infinite love! A God to sacrifice His blood and His life! And for whom? For His ungrateful creatures; dying in an ocean

---

[222] John 19:30.

of sufferings and shame in order to pay the penalty due to their sins. Ah, infinite goodness! O infinite love!

O my Jesus! You are, then, dead, on account of the love which You have borne me! Oh, let me never again live, even for a single moment, without loving You! I love You, my chief and only good; I love You, my Jesus—dead for me! O my sorrowing Mother Mary, help a servant of yours, who desires to love Jesus.

Meditation 45: Good Friday

Jesus Hanging Dead upon the Cross

Raise up thine eyes, my soul, and behold that crucified man. Behold the divine Lamb now sacrificed upon that altar of pain. Consider that He is the beloved Son of the Eternal Father, and consider that He is dead for the love that He has borne you. See how He holds His arms stretched out to embrace you; His head bent down to give the kiss of peace; His side open to receive you into His heart. What do you say? Does not a God so loving deserve to be loved? Listen to the words He addresses to you from that cross: "Look, My son, and see whether there be anyone in the world who has loved you more than I have."

No, my God, there is none that has loved me more than You. But what return shall I ever be able to make to a God who has been willing to die for me? What love from a creature will ever be able to recompense the love of his Creator, who died to gain his love?

O God, had the vilest one of mankind suffered for me what Jesus Christ has suffered, could I ever refrain from loving Him? Were I to see any man torn to pieces with scourges and fastened to a cross in order to save my life, could I ever bear it in mind without feeling a tender emotion of love? And were there to be brought to me the portrait of him, as he lay dead upon the cross, could I behold it with an eye of indifference when I considered: "This man is dead, tortured thus, for love of me. Had he not loved me, he would not so have died."

Ah, my Redeemer, O love of my soul! How shall I ever again be able to forget You? How shall I ever be able to think that my sins have reduced You so low, and not always bewail the wrongs that I have done to Your goodness? How shall I ever be able to see You dead of pain on this cross for love of me and not love You to the uttermost of my power?

O my dear Redeemer, well do I recognize in these Your wounds, and in Your lacerated body, as it were through so many lattices, the tender affection which You retain for me. Since, then, in order to pardon me, You have not pardoned Yourself, oh, look upon me now with the same love wherewith You one day looked upon me from the cross, while You were dying for me. Look upon me and enlighten me, and draw my whole heart to Yourself so that, from this day forth, I may love no one else but You. Let me not ever be unmindful of Your death. You promised that, when raised up upon the cross, You would draw all our hearts to You. Behold this heart of mine, which, made tender by Your death, and enamored of You, desires to offer no further resistance to Your calls. Oh, draw it to Yourself, and make it all Your own! You have died for me, and I desire to die for You, and if I continue to live, I will live for You alone. O pains of Jesus, O ignominies of Jesus, O death of Jesus, O love of Jesus, fix yourselves within my heart, and let the remembrance of you abide there always, to be continually smiting me and inflaming me with love. I love You, O infinite goodness; I love You, O infinite love. You are, and shall ever be, my one and only love. O Mary, Mother of love, obtain love for me.

MARY PRESENT ON CALVARY

There stood by the cross of Jesus His Mother.[223] We observe in this the Queen of Martyrs, a sort of martyrdom more cruel than any other martyrdom—that of a mother so placed as to behold an innocent Son executed upon a gibbet of infamy: "she stood." Ever since Jesus was apprehended in the garden, He has been abandoned by His disciples, but Mary abandons Him not. She stays with Him till she sees Him expire before her eyes: "she stood close by." Mothers, in general, flee away from the presence of their sons when they see them suffer and cannot render them any assistance: content enough would they be themselves to endure their sons' sufferings, and therefore, when they see them suffering without the power of succoring them, they have not the strength to endure so great a pain and consequently flee away and go to a distance. Not so Mary. She sees her Son in torments;

---

[223]   John 19:25.

she sees that the pains are taking His life away, but she flees not, nor moves to a distance. On the contrary, she draws near to the cross whereon her Son is dying. O sorrowing Mary, disdain me not for a companion to assist at the death of your Jesus and mine.

She stood near to the cross. The cross, then, is the bed whereon Jesus leaves His life, a bed of suffering where this afflicted Mother is watching Jesus, all wounded as He is with scourges and with thorns. Mary observes how this her poor Son, suspended from those three iron nails, finds neither a position nor repose. She would wish to give Him some relief; she would wish, at least, since He has to die, to have Him die in her arms. But nothing of all this is allowed here. "Ah, cross!" she says. "Give me back my Son! You are a malefactor's gibbet, whereas my Son is innocent." But grieve not yourself, O Mother. It is the will of the eternal Father that the cross should not give Jesus back to you until after He has died and breathed His last. O Queen of Sorrows, obtain for me sorrow for my sins.

There stood by the cross His Mother! Meditate, my soul, upon Mary as she stands at the foot of the cross watching her Son. Her Son—but, O God, what a Son—a Son who was, at one and the same time, her Son and her God, a Son who had from all eternity chosen her to be His Mother, and had given her a preference in His love before all mankind and all the angels! A Son so beautiful, so holy, and so lovely; a Son who had been ever obedient unto her; a Son who was her one and only love, being as He was both her Son and God. And this Mother had to see such a Son die of pain before her very eyes!

O Mary, O Mother, most afflicted of all mothers! I compassionate your heart, more especially when you beheld your Jesus surrender Himself upon the cross, open His mouth, and expire; for love of this your Son, now dead for my salvation, recommend unto Him my soul. My Jesus, for the sake of the merits of Mary's sorrows, have mercy upon me, and grant me the grace of dying for You, as You have died for me: "May I die, O my Lord" (will I say unto You, with Saint Francis of Assisi), "for love of the love of You, who have vouchsafed to die for love of the love of me."

EASTER
MEDITATIONS

THE JOYS OF HEAVEN

O h, happy are we if we suffer with patience on earth the troubles of this present life! Distress of circumstances, fears, bodily infirmities, persecutions, and crosses of every kind will one day all come to an end, and if we be saved, they will all become for us subjects of joy and glory in paradise: *Your sorrow* (says the Savior, to encourage us) *shall be turned into joy.*[224] So great are the delights of paradise that they can neither be explained nor understood by us mortals: *Eye has not seen* (says the Apostle), *nor ear heard, neither has it entered into the heart of man, what things God has prepared for those who love Him.*[225] Beauties like the beauties of paradise, eye has never seen; harmonies like unto the harmonies of paradise, ear has never heard; nor has ever human heart gained the comprehension of the joys which God has prepared for those that love Him. Beautiful is the sight of a

---

[224] John 16:20.
[225] 1 Cor. 2:9.

landscape adorned with hills, plains, woods, and views of the sea. Beautiful is the sight of a garden abounding with fruit, flowers, and fountains. Oh, how much more beautiful is paradise!

To understand how great the joys of paradise are, it is enough to know that in that blessed realm resides a God omnipotent, whose care is to render happy His beloved souls. Saint Bernard says that paradise is a place where "there is nothing that you would not, and everything that you would." There you shall not find anything displeasing to yourself, and everything you desire you shall find: "There is nothing that you would not." In paradise there is no night; no seasons of winter and summer, but one perpetual day of unvaried serenity, and one perpetual spring of unvaried delight. No more persecutions, no jealousies are there; for there do all in sincerity love one another, and each rejoices in each other's good as if it were his own. No more bodily infirmities, no pains are there, for the body is no longer subject to suffering; no poverty is there, for everyone is rich to the full, not having anything more to desire; no more fears are there, for the soul being confirmed in grace can sin no more, nor lose that supreme good which it possesses.

"There is everything that you would." In paradise you shall have whatsoever you desire. There the sight is satisfied in beholding that city so beautiful, and its citizens all clothed in royal apparel, for they are all kings of that everlasting kingdom. There shall we see the beauty of Mary, whose appearance will be more beautiful than that of all the angels and saints together. We shall see the beauty of Jesus, which will immeasurably surpass the beauty of Mary. The smell will be satisfied with the perfumes of paradise. The hearing will be satisfied with the harmonies of heaven and the canticles of the blessed, who will all with ravishing sweetness sing the divine praises for all eternity.

Ah, my God, I deserve not paradise, but hell; yet Your death gives me a hope of obtaining it. I desire and ask paradise of You, not so much in order to enjoy as in order to love You everlastingly, secure that it will never more be possible for me to lose You. O Mary, my Mother, O Star of the Sea, it is for you, by your prayers, to conduct me to paradise.

THE SOUL THAT LEAVES THIS LIFE IN THE STATE OF GRACE

Let us imagine to ourselves a soul that, on departing out of this world, enters eternity in the grace of God. All full of humility and of confidence, it presents itself before Jesus, its judge and Savior. Jesus embraces it, gives it His benediction, and causes it to hear those words of sweetness: *Come, My spouse, come, you shall be crowned.*[226] If the soul has need of being purified, He sends it to purgatory, and all resigned, it embraces the chastisement because it itself wishes not to enter into heaven, that land of purity, if it is not wholly purified. The guardian angel comes to conduct it to purgatory; it first returns him thanks for the assistance he has rendered it in its lifetime and then obediently follows him.

---

[226] Cant. 4:8.

Ah, my God, when will that day arrive on which I shall see myself out of this world of perils, secure of never being able to lose You anymore? Yes, willingly will I go to the purgatory which shall be mine; joyfully will I embrace all its pains; sufficient will it be for me in that fire to love You with all my heart, since there I shall love no one else but You.

The purgation over, the angel will return and say to it, "Come along, beautiful soul, the punishment is at an end; come, and enjoy the presence of your God, who is awaiting you in paradise." Behold, the soul now passes beyond the clouds, passes beyond the spheres and the stars, and enters into heaven. O God, what will it say on entering into that beautiful country, and casting its first glance on that city of delights? The angels and saints, and especially its own holy advocates, will go to meet it, and with jubilation will they welcome it, saying, "Welcome, O companion of our own; welcome!" Ah, my Jesus, make me worthy of it.

What consolation will it not feel in meeting there with relatives and friends of its own who have previously entered into heaven! But greater by far will be its joy in beholding Mary its Queen, and in kissing her feet, while it will thank her for the many kindnesses she has done it. The Queen will embrace it, and will herself present it unto Jesus, who will receive it as a spouse. And Jesus will then present it to His divine Father, who will embrace and bless it, saying, *Enter into the joy of your Lord.*[227] And thus will He beatify it with the same beatitude that He

---

[227]   Matt. 25:21.

Himself enjoys. Ah, my God, make me love You exceedingly in this life, that I may love You exceedingly in eternity. You are the object most worthy of being loved; You deserve all my love; I will love none but You. Do You help me by Your grace. And Mary, my Mother, be my protectress.

MEDITATION 3: EASTER TUESDAY

THE HAPPINESS OF HEAVEN

The beauties of the saints, the heavenly music, and all the other delights of paradise form but the lesser portion of its treasures. The possession which gives to the soul its fullness of bliss is that of seeing a loving God face to face. Saint Augustine says that were God to let His beautiful face be seen by the damned, hell with all its torments would become to them a paradise. Even in this world, when God gives a soul in prayer a taste of His sweet presence, and by a ray of light discovers to it His goodness and the love which He bears it, so great is the contentment that the soul feels itself dissolve and melt away in love, and yet, in this life, it is not possible for us to see God as He is; we behold Him obscured, as if through a thick veil. What, then, will it be when God shall take away that veil from before us and shall cause us to behold Him face to face openly?

O Lord, for having turned my back upon You, no more should I be worthy to behold You, but, relying on Your goodness,

I hope to see You and to love You in paradise forever. I speak thus because I am speaking with a God who has died in order to give paradise to me.

Although the souls that love God are the most happy in this world, yet they cannot, here below, enjoy a happiness full and complete; that fear, which arises from not knowing whether they be deserving of the love or the hatred of their beloved Savior, keeps them, as it were, in perpetual suffering. But in paradise the soul is certain that it loves God and is loved by God, and it sees that that sweet tie of love which holds it united with God will never be loosened throughout all eternity. The flames of its love will be increased by the clearer knowledge which the soul will then possess of what the love of God has been in being made man, and having willed to die for it, and in having, moreover, given Himself to it in the sacrament of the Eucharist. Its love will be increased by then beholding, in all their distinctness, the graces which He has given it in order to lead it to heaven; it will see that the crosses sent to it in life have all been artifices of His love to render it happy. It will see, besides, the mercies He has granted it, the many lights and calls to penance. From the summit of that blessed Mount will it behold the many lost souls now in hell for sins less than its own, and it will behold itself now saved, possessed of God, and certain that it can nevermore lose Him throughout all eternity. My Jesus, my Jesus, when will that too happy day for me arrive?

The happiness of the blessed soul will be perfected by knowing with absolute certainty that God whom it then enjoys it will have to enjoy for all eternity. Were there to be any fear in the blessed that they might lose that God whom they now enjoy, paradise would no more be paradise. But no; the blessed soul is certain, with the certainty which it has of the existence of God, that supreme good which it enjoys, it will enjoy forever. That joy, moreover, will not grow less with time; it will be ever new. The blessed one will be ever happy and ever thirsting for that happiness, and on the other hand, while ever thirsting, will be ever satiated. When, therefore, we see ourselves afflicted with the troubles of this life, let us lift up our eyes unto heaven and console ourselves by saying, paradise. The sufferings will one day come to an end; nay, they will themselves become objects over which to rejoice. The saints await us; the angels await us; Mary awaits us; and Jesus stands with the crown in His hand wherewith to crown us if we shall be faithful to Him.

Ah, my God, when will come that day on which I shall arrive at possessing You and be able to say unto You, my love, I cannot lose You anymore? O Mary, my hope, never cease from praying for me, until you see me safe at your feet in paradise!

MEDITATION 4: EASTER WEDNESDAY

THE HOPE OF SALVATION

Oh, how great is the hope of salvation which the death of Jesus Christ imparts to us: *Who is He that shall condemn? Christ Jesus who died, who also makes intercession for us.*[228] Who is it, asks the Apostle, that has to condemn us? It is that same Redeemer who, in order not to condemn us to eternal death, condemned Himself to a cruel death upon a cross. From this Saint Thomas of Villanova encourages us, saying, "What are you afraid of, sinner? How shall He condemn you penitent, who dies that you may not be condemned? How shall He cast you off returning, who came from heaven seeking you?"[229] But greater still is the encouragement given us by this same Savior of ours when, speaking by Isaiah, He says, *Behold, I have graven you upon My hands; your walls are always before My eyes.*[230] Be not distrustful,

---

228 Rom. 8:34.
229 *Tractatus de Adventu Domini.*
230 Is. 49:16.

My sheep; see how much you cost Me. I keep you engraved upon My hands in these wounds which I have suffered for you; these are ever reminding Me to help you and to defend you from your enemies: love Me and have confidence.

Yes, my Jesus, I love You and feel confidence in You. To rescue me, this has cost You dear; to save me will cost You nothing. It is Your will that all should be saved and that none should perish. If my sins cause me to dread, Your goodness reassures me, more desirous as You are to do me good than I am to receive it. Ah, my beloved Redeemer, I will say to You with Job: *Even though You should kill me, yet I will hope in You . . . and You will be my Savior.*[231] Were You even to drive me away from Your presence, O my love, yet I would not leave off from hoping in You, who are my Savior. Too much do these wounds of Yours and this blood encourage me to hope for every good from Your mercy. I love You, O dear Jesus; I love You, and I hope.

The glorious Saint Bernard one day, in sickness, saw himself before the judgment-seat of God, where the devil was accusing him of his sins and telling him that he did not deserve paradise: "It is true that I deserve not paradise," the saint replied, "but Jesus has a twofold title to this kingdom—in the first place, as being by nature Son of God, in the next place, as having purchased it by His death. He contents Himself with the first of these, and the second He makes over to me, and therefore it is that I ask and hope for paradise." We, too, can say the same; for Saint Paul

---

[231]   See Job 13:15–16.

tells us that the will of Jesus Christ to die, consumed by sufferings, had for its end the obtaining of paradise for all sinners that are penitent and resolved to amend: *And, being perfected, He was made the cause of eternal salvation to all that obey Him.*[232] And hence the Apostle subjoins: *Let us run to the fight proposed unto us, looking on Jesus, the Author and Finisher of faith, who, having joy proposed unto Him, underwent the cross, despising the shame.*[233] Let us go forth with courage to fight against our enemies, fixing our eyes on Jesus Christ, who, together with the merits of His passion, offers us the victory and the crown.

[232] Heb. 5:9.
[233] Heb. 12:1–2.

THE GRACES FROM THE PASSION

Saint Leo declares that Jesus Christ, by His death, has brought us more good than the devil brought us evil in the sin of Adam: "We have gained greater things through the grace of Christ than we had lost through the envy of the devil."[234] And this the Apostle distinctly says when writing to the Romans: *Not as the offence, so also is the gift. . . . Where the offence abounded, grace did super-abound.*[235] Cardinal Hugh explains it: "The grace of Christ is of greater efficacy than is the offence." There is no comparison, says the Apostle, between the sins of man and the gift which God has made us in giving us Jesus Christ; great as was the sin of Adam, much greater by far was the grace which Jesus Christ, by His passion, merited for us: *I have come that*

---

234   *De Ascensione Domini*, sermo 1.
235   Rom. 5:15, 20.

they may have life, and that they may have it more abundantly.[236] I am come into the world, the Savior protests, to the end that mankind, who were dead through sin, may receive through Me not only the life of grace but a life yet more abundant than that which they had lost by sin. Wherefore it is that Holy Church calls the sin happy which has merited to have such a Redeemer: "O happy fault, which deserved such and so great a Redeemer."[237]

Behold, God is my Savior, I will deal confidently, and will not fear.[238] If, then, O my Jesus, You, who are an omnipotent God, are also my Savior, what fear shall I have of being damned? If, in time past, I have offended You, I repent of it with all my heart. From this time forth I wish to serve You, to obey You, and to love You. I firmly hope that You, my Redeemer, who have done and suffered so much for my salvation, will not deny me any grace that I shall need in order to be saved: "I will act with confidence, firmly hoping that nothing necessary to salvation will be denied me by Him who has done and suffered so much for my salvation."

You shall draw water from the fountains of the Savior, and you shall say in that day, Praise the Lord, and call upon His name.[239] The wounds of Jesus Christ are now the blessed fountains from which we can draw forth all graces if we pray unto Him with faith: *And a fountain shall come forth from the house of the Lord,*

---

[236] John 10:10.
[237] *Exsultet.*
[238] Is. 12:2.
[239] Is. 12:3–4.

and shall water the torrent of thorns.[240] The death of Jesus, says Isaiah, is precisely this promised fountain, which has bathed our souls in the water of grace and, from being thorns of sins, has, by His merits, transformed them into flowers and fruits of life eternal. He, the loving Redeemer, made Himself, as Saint Paul tells us, poor in this world in order that we, through the merit of His poverty, might become rich: *For your sakes He became poor, that, through His poverty, you might be rich.*[241] By reason of sin we were ignorant, unjust, wicked, slaves of hell, but Jesus Christ, says the Apostle, by dying and making satisfaction for us, *is by God made for us Wisdom, Justice, Sanctification, and Redemption.*[242] That is to say, as Saint Bernard explains it, "Wisdom, in His preaching, justice in His absolving, sanctification in His conduct, redemption in His passion"[243] He has made Himself our wisdom by instructing us, our justice by pardoning us, our sanctity by His example, and our redemption by His passion, delivering us from the hands of Lucifer. In short, as Saint Paul says, the merits of Jesus Christ have enriched us with all good things so that we no more want for anything in order to be able to receive all graces: *In all things you are made rich . . . so that nothing is wanting to you in any grace.*[244]

---

[240] Joel 3:18.
[241] 2 Cor. 8:9.
[242] 1 Cor. 1:30.
[243] *In Canticum Canticorum,* sermo 22.
[244] 1 Cor. 1:5, 7.

MEDITATION 6: EASTER FRIDAY

THE ETERNAL FATHER'S LOVE

God so loved the world, that He gave His only begotten Son.[245]
God, says Jesus Christ, has loved the world to that degree
that He has given it His own and only Son. In this gift there
are three things demanding our consideration: Who is the giver,
what is the thing given, and the greatness of the love wherewith
He gives it? We are already aware that the more exalted the donor is, the more to be prized is the gift. One who receives a flower from a monarch will set a higher value on that flower than
on a large amount of money. How much ought we not, then, to
prize this gift, coming to us as it does from the hands of one who
is God! And what is it that He has given us? His own Son. The
love of this God did not content itself with having given us so
many good things on this earth, until it had reached the point
of giving us its whole self in the person of the Incarnate Word:

---

[245] John 3:16.

"He gave us not a servant, not an Angel, but His own Son,"[246] says Saint John Chrysostom. Wherefore Holy Church exultingly exclaims, "O wondrous condescension of Your mercy in our regard! O unappreciable love of charity! That You might redeem a slave, You delivered up Your Son."[247]

O infinite God, how could You condescend to exercise towards us so wondrous a compassion! Who shall ever be able to understand an excess so great as that, in order to ransom the slave, You were willing to give us Your only Son? Ah, my kindest Lord, since You have given me the best that You have, it is but just that I should give You the most that I can. You desire my love: of You I desire nothing else, but only Your love. Behold this miserable heart of mine; I consecrate it wholly to Your love. Depart from my heart, all you creatures; give room to my God, who deserves and desires to possess it wholly and without companions. I love You, O God of love; I love You above everything, and I desire to love You alone, my Creator, my treasure, my all.

God has given us His Son, and why? For love alone. Pilate, for fear of men, gave Jesus up to the Jews: *He delivered Him up to their will.*[248] But the Eternal Father gave His Son to us for the love which He bore us: *He delivered Him up for us all.*[249] Saint Thomas says that "love has the nature of a first gift."[250] When a

---

[246]   *In Joannem*, homilia 26.
[247]   *Exsultet.*
[248]   Luke 23:25.
[249]   Rom. 8:32.
[250]   *S. T.*, I, q. 38, a. 2.

present is made us, the first gift that we receive is that of the love which the donor offers us in the thing that he gives: because, observes the Angelic Doctor, the one and only reason of every voluntary gift is love; otherwise, when a gift is made for some other end than that of simple affection, the gift can no longer rightly be called a true gift. The gift which the Eternal Father made us of His Son was a true gift, perfectly voluntary, and without any merit of ours, and therefore it is said that the Incarnation of the Word was effected through the operation of the Holy Spirit: that is, through love alone; as the same holy Doctor says: "Through God's supreme love it was brought to pass that the Son of God assumed to Himself flesh."[251]

But not only was it out of pure love that God gave unto us His Son, He also gave Him to us with an immensity of love. This is precisely what Jesus wished to signify when He said: *God so loved the world.*[252] The word "so" (says Saint John Chrysostom) signifies the magnitude of the love wherewith God made us this great gift: "The word 'so' signifies the vehemence of the love."[253]

---

[251] *S. T.,* III, q. 32. a. 1.
[252] John 3:16.
[253] *In Joannem,* homilia 26.

THE BURIAL AND RESURRECTION OF JESUS CHRIST

Jesus came into the world, not only to redeem us, but by His own example to teach us all virtues, and especially humility and holy poverty, which is inseparably united with humility. On this account He chose to be born in a cave; to live, a poor man, in a workshop for thirty years; and finally to die, poor and naked, upon a cross, seeing His garments divided among the soldiers before He breathed His last; while after His death He was compelled to receive His winding-sheet for burial as an alms from others. Let the poor be consoled, thus seeing Jesus Christ, the King of heaven and earth, thus living and dying in poverty in order to enrich us with His merits and gifts; as the Apostle says, *For your sake He became poor, when He was rich, that by His poverty you might be rich.*[254] For this cause the saints, to become like Jesus in His poverty, have despised all earthly riches and honors, that they might go one day to enjoy with Jesus Christ the riches and honors prepared by God in heaven for them that love Him; of which blessings the Apostle says that *eye has not seen, nor ear heard, nor has it entered into the mind of man to conceive what God has prepared for them that love Him.*[255]

Jesus Christ, then, rose with the glory of possessing all power in heaven and earth, not as God alone, but as a man; wherefore all angels and men are subject to Him. Let us rejoice in thus seeing in glory our Savior, our Father, and the best friend that we possess. And let us rejoice for ourselves, because the resurrection of Jesus Christ is for us a sure pledge of our own resurrection, and of the glory that we hope one day to have in heaven, both in soul and in body. This hope gave courage to the holy martyrs to suffer with gladness all the evils of this life and the most cruel torments of tyrants. We must rest assured, however, that none will rejoice with Jesus Christ but he who is willing to suffer in this world with Him; nor will he obtain the crown who does not fight as he ought to fight. *He that strives in a wrestling is not crowned unless he has striven lawfully.*[256] At the same time let us be sure of what the same Apostle says, that all the sufferings of this life are short and light in comparison with the boundless

---

[254]   2 Cor. 8:9.
[255]   1 Cor. 2:9.
[256]   2 Tim. 2:5.

and eternal joys which we hope to enjoy in paradise.[257] Let us labor the more to continue in the grace of God, and continually to pray for perseverance in His favor; for without prayer, and that persevering, we shall not obtain this perseverance, and without perseverance, we shall not obtain salvation.

O sweet Jesus, worthy of all love, how have You so loved men that in order to show Your love, You have not refused to die wounded and dishonored upon an infamous tree! O my God, how is it that there are so few among men who love You with their heart? O my dear Redeemer, of these few I would be one! Miserable that I am, for my past life I have forgotten Your love and given up Your grace for miserable pleasures. I know the evil I have done; I grieve for it with all my heart; I would die for grief. Now, O my beloved Redeemer, I love You more than myself, and I am ready to die a thousand times rather than lose Your friendship. I thank You for the light You have given me. O my Jesus, my hope, leave me not in my own hands; help me until my death.

O Mary, Mother of God, pray to Jesus for me.

---

[257] See 2 Cor. 4:17.

MEDITATION 8: DIVINE MERCY SUNDAY

JESUS CRUCIFIED IS OUR ONLY HOPE

There is no salvation in any other.[258] Saint Peter says that all our salvation is in Jesus Christ, who, by means of the cross, where He sacrificed His life for us, opened us a way for hoping for every blessing from God if we would be faithful to His commands.

Let us hear what Saint John Chrysostom says of the cross: "The cross is the hope of Christians, the staff of the lame, the comfort of the poor, the destruction of the proud, the victory over the devils, the guide of youth, the rudder of sailors, the refuge of those who are in danger, the counsellor of the just, the rest of the afflicted, the physician of the sick, the glory of martyrs."[259] The cross—that is, Jesus crucified—is:

---

[258] Acts 4:12.
[259] *Homilia de Cruce.*

The *hope* of the faithful, because if we had not Jesus Christ we should have no hope of salvation.

It is the *staff* of the lame, because we are all lame in our present state of corruption. We have no strength to walk in the way of salvation except that which is communicated to us by the grace of Jesus Christ.

It is the *comfort* of the poor, which we all are, for all we have we have from Jesus Christ.

It is the *destruction* of the proud, for the followers of the Crucified cannot be proud, seeing Him dead as a malefactor upon the cross.

It is *victory* over the devils, for the very sign of the cross is sufficient to drive them from us.

It is the *instructor* of the young, for admirable is the teaching which they who are beginning to walk in the ways of God learn from the cross.

It is the *rudder* of mariners, and guides us through the storms of this present life.

It is the *refuge* of those in danger, for they who are in peril of perishing, through temptations of strong passions, find a secure harbor by flying to the cross.

It is the *counsellor* of the just, for how many saints learn wisdom from the cross—that is, from the troubles of this life.

It is the *rest* of the afflicted, for where can they find greater relief than in contemplating the cross, on which a God suffers for love of them?

It is the *physician* of the sick, for when they embrace it, they are healed of the wounds of the soul.

It is the *glory* of martyrs, for to be made like Jesus Christ, the King of Martyrs, is the greatest glory they can possess.

In a word, all our hopes are placed in the merits of Jesus Christ. The Apostle says, *I know how to be humbled, and I know how to abound . . . how to be satisfied, and how to hunger; how to abound, and how to suffer poverty. I can do all things in Him who strengthens me.*[260] (In the Greek text, *In Christ who is strengthening me.*) Thus Saint Paul, instructed by the Lord, says, I know how I ought to conduct myself: when God humbles me, I resign myself to His will; when He exalts me, to Him I give all the honor; when He gives me abundance, I thank Him; when He makes me endure poverty, still I bless Him; and I do all this not by my own strength, but by the strength of the grace which God gives me. For he that trusts in Jesus Christ is strengthened with invincible power.

The Lord, says Saint Bernard, makes those who hope in Him all-powerful. The saint also adds that a soul which does not presume upon its own strength but is strengthened by the Word can govern itself so that no evil shall have power over it and that no force, no fraud, no snare can cast it down.[261]

[260] Phil. 4:12–13.
[261] *In Canticum Canticorum*, sermo 85.

APPENDIX

PRAYER TO JESUS CRUCIFIED

By Saint Alphonsus de Liguori

My crucified Love, and my most sweet Jesus, I believe in You, and confess You to be the true Son of God and Savior of the world! I adore You from the abyss of my misery, and thank You for the death which You suffered to obtain for me the life of divine grace. O most faithful of all friends! O most loving of all fathers! O kindest of all masters! My beloved Redeemer, to You I am indebted for my salvation, for my soul, my body, and my whole self. You have delivered me from hell; through You I have received the pardon of my sins; through You do I hope for paradise. But my ingratitude is so great that, instead of loving You, after so many mercies and special endearments of love, I have only offended You afresh. I confess that I deserve not to be allowed to love You any more. But no, my Jesus, choose some other punishment for me, and not this. If I have despised You up to this time, now I love You, and I desire to love You with all my heart. You know very well that without Your help I can do nothing. Since, then, You command me to love You and offer me Your grace, provided I ask it in Your name, confiding in Your goodness and in the promise You have made me, saying, *Whatsoever you shall ask the Father in My name, that I will do,*[262] I present myself, poor as I am, before the throne of Your mercy, and by the merits of Your passion, I ask You first to pardon all my sins, of which I repent with all my soul, because by them I have offended You, who are infinite goodness. Pardon me, then, and at the same time, give me holy perseverance till death; grant me also the gift of Your holy love.

Ah, my Jesus, my hope, and my only love! My life, my treasure, my all! Shed over my soul that light of truth and that fire of love which You came to bring into the world. Enlighten me to know every day better why You should be loved, and to see the immense love You have shown me in suffering and dying for me. Ah, grant that the same love may be in me as that with which Your eternal Father loves You. And as He is in You, and is one with You, so may I, by means of a true love, be in You, and by a perfect union of will, become one with You. Grant me, then, O my Jesus, the grace of loving You with all my affections, that I may love You always and ever beg the grace to love You so that, ending my life in Your love, I may come to love You in heaven with a purer and more perfect love, never to cease loving You, and to possess You for all eternity!

---

[262] John 14:14.

O Mother of beautiful love, most blessed Virgin, my advocate, my Mother, my hope after Jesus—who are of all creatures the most loving towards God and desire nothing but that He should be loved by all—ah, for the love of this Son dying before your eyes for my salvation, pray for me and obtain for me the grace to love Him always and with all my heart! I ask it of you, and from you do I hope to obtain it. Amen.

Prayer to Jesus

By the Merit of Each Particular Pain Which He suffered in His Passion

By Saint Alphonsus de Liguori

O my Jesus, by that humiliation which You practiced in washing the feet of Your disciples, I pray You to bestow upon me the grace of true humility, that I may humble myself to all, especially to such as treat me with contempt.

My Jesus, by that sorrow which You suffered in the garden, sufficient, as it was, to cause Your death, I pray You to deliver me from the sorrow of hell, from living for evermore at a distance from You, and without the power of ever loving You again.

My Jesus, by that horror which You had of my sins, which were then present to Your sight, give me a true sorrow for all the offenses which I have committed against You.

My Jesus, by that pain which You experienced at seeing Yourself betrayed by Judas with a kiss, give me the grace to be ever faithful unto You, and nevermore to betray You, as I have done in time past.

My Jesus, by that pain which You felt at seeing Yourself bound like a culprit to be taken before the judges, I pray You to bind me to Yourself by the sweet chains of holy love so that I may nevermore see myself separated from You, my only good.

My Jesus, by all those insults, buffetings, and spittings which You on that night suffered in the house of Caiaphas, give me the strength to suffer in peace, for love of You, all the affronts which I shall meet with from men.

My Jesus, by that ridicule which You received from Herod in being treated as a fool, give me the grace to endure with patience all that men shall say of me, treating me as base, senseless, or wicked.

My Jesus, by that outrage which You received from the Jews in seeing Yourself placed after Barabbas, give me the grace to suffer with patience the dishonor of seeing myself placed after others.

My Jesus, by that pain which You suffered in Your most holy body when You were so cruelly scourged, give me the grace to suffer with patience all the pains of my sicknesses, and especially those of my death.

My Jesus, by that pain which You suffered in Your most sacred head when it was pierced with the thorns, give me the grace never to consent to thoughts displeasing unto You.

My Jesus, by that act of Yours by which You accepted the death of the cross, to which Pilate condemned You, give me the grace to accept my death with resignation, together with all the other pains which shall accompany it.

My Jesus, by the pain which You suffered in carrying Your cross on Your journey to Calvary, give me the grace to suffer with patience all my crosses in this life.

My Jesus, by that pain which You suffered in having the nails driven through Your hands and Your feet, I pray You to nail my will unto Your feet so that I may will nothing save that which You will.

My Jesus, by the affliction which You suffered in having gall given You to drink, give me the grace not to offend You by intemperance in eating and drinking.

My Jesus, by that pain which You experienced in taking leave of Your holy Mother upon the cross, deliver me from an inordinate love for my relatives, or for any other creature, so that my heart may be wholly and always Yours.

My Jesus, by that desolation which You suffered in Your death in seeing Yourself abandoned by Your Eternal Father, give me the grace to suffer all my desolations with patience, without ever losing my confidence in Your goodness.

My Jesus, by those three hours of affliction and agony which You suffered when dying upon the cross, give me the grace to suffer with resignation, for love of You, the pains of my agony at the hour of death.

My Jesus, by that great sorrow which You felt when Your most holy soul, when You were expiring, separated itself from Your most sacred body, give me the grace to breathe forth my soul in the hour of my death, offering up my sorrow then to You, together with an act of perfect love, so that I may go to love You in heaven, face to face, with all my strength and for all eternity.

And you, most holy Virgin, and my Mother Mary, by that sword which pierced your heart when you beheld your Son bow down His head and expire, I pray to assist me in the hour of my death so that I may come to praise you and to thank you in paradise for all the graces that you have obtained for me from God.

The Clock of the Passion

P.M.	
5 to 7	Jesus, having taken leave of Mary, celebrates His last supper.
8	Jesus washes the feet of the apostles, and institutes the Most Holy Sacrament.
9	Discourse of Jesus; He goes to the Garden of Olives.
10	Prayer of Jesus in the garden.
11	Agony.
Midnight	The sweating of blood.
1	Jesus is betrayed by Judas and is bound.
2	Jesus is led before Annas.
3	Jesus is taken before Caiaphas and receives a blow in the face.
4	Jesus is blindfolded, struck, and scoffed at.
5	Jesus is led to the council and declared guilty of death.

6	Jesus is taken to Pilate and accused.
7	Jesus is mocked by Herod.
8	Jesus is conducted to Pilate, and Barabbas is preferred to Him.
9	Jesus is scourged at the pillar.
10	Jesus is crowned with thorns and exhibited to the people.
11	Jesus is condemned to death and goes to Calvary.
Midday	Jesus is stripped and crucified.
1	Jesus prays for His murderers.
2	Jesus recommends His spirit to His Father.
3	Jesus dies.
4	Jesus is pierced with a lance.
5	Jesus is taken down from the cross and delivered over to His Mother.
6	Jesus is buried and left in the sepulcher.